DIAMOND COVE

Harcourt Brace & Company

DIAMOND COVE

Senior Authors
Roger C. Farr
Dorothy S. Strickland

Authors
Richard F. Abrahamson ◆ Alma Flor Ada ◆ Barbara Bowen Coulter
Bernice E. Cullinan ◆ Margaret A. Gallego
W. Dorsey Hammond
Nancy Roser ◆ Junko Yokota ◆ Hallie Kay Yopp

Senior Consultant
Asa G. Hilliard III

Consultants
Lee Bennett Hopkins ◆ Stephen Krashen ◆ David A. Monti ◆ Rosalia Salinas

Harcourt Brace & Company
Orlando Atlanta Austin Boston San Francisco Chicago Dallas New York Toronto London

Requests for permission to make copies of any part of the work should be mailed to the following address: School Permissions, Harcourt Brace & Company, 6277 Sea Harbor Drive, Orlando, Florida 32887-6777.

HARCOURT BRACE and Quill Design is a registered trademark of Harcourt Brace & Company.

Acknowledgments appear in the back of this work.

Printed in the United States of America

ISBN 0-15-310109-1

3 4 5 6 7 8 9 10   048   2000 99

Dear Reader,

Imagine that you have discovered a special place, like the castle on the cover of this book. It is a place to explore, a place to build, and a place to enjoy the natural world.

This book, **Diamond Cove**, is like a special place. In these pages, you can meet new people and learn about how nature stays in balance. You can travel to new communities, such as Ayutla in Mexico, Harlem in New York City, and Henson Creek in the Blue Ridge Mountains. In **Diamond Cove**, you can build new friendships and new understandings. You can do all of this while enjoying wonderful stories, poems, and articles.

Welcome to **Diamond Cove**! Perhaps you will make some discoveries here that nobody else has made.

Sincerely,

The Authors

The Authors

THE BALANCE OF NATURE

CONTENTS

PAULA DANZIGER
AMBER BROWN
IS NOT A CRAYON

Grandfather's Journey

ALLEN SAY

MY GREAT-AUNT
ARIZONA

BY
GLORIA HOUSTON ★ ILLUSTRATED BY
SUSAN CONDIE LAMB

SHERRY GARLAND

THE
LOTUS
SEED

TATSURO KIUCHI

When Jo Louis
Won the Title

Belinda Rochelle Illustrated by Larry Johnson

Traveling to New Communities

CONTENTS

9

Exploring Challenges

CONTENTS

11

THE BALANCE OF
NATURE

Some animals are cute and cuddly, and others are wild and dangerous. All animals, and all other parts of nature, are important. In this theme you will find out how nature keeps a balance between all living things.

THE BALANCE OF
NATURE

CONTENTS

All About Alligators

written and illustrated by Jim Arnosky

Learn what alligators look like, where they live, how they move, what they eat, and how dangerous they are.

SLJ Best Books;
Outstanding Science Trade Book

Signatures Library

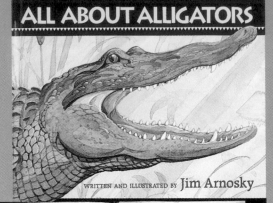

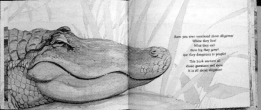

Dolphin Adventure: A True Story

by Wayne Grover

A dolphin family turns to a human diver for help in this exciting true story.

Outstanding Science Trade Book

Signatures Library

When Hunger Calls
by Bert Kitchen

Each different kind of animal has its own special skills for catching its dinner.

A Journey of Hope /Una Jornada de Esperanza
by Bob Harvey and Diane Kelsay Harvey

A baby sea turtle makes her way from the nest to the sea, in a journey filled with danger.

Outstanding Science Trade Book

A JOURNEY OF HOPE
UNA JORNADA DE ESPERANZA

Text and Photography by
Bob Harvey & Diane Kelsay Harvey
Illustrations by Carol Johnson

The Year of the Panda
by Miriam Schlein

Lu Yi helps to rescue a panda, and in the process he discovers a possible career for the future.

Outstanding Science Trade Book

Borreguita

Borreguita and the Coyote

SLJ Best Books
Notable Trade Book
in Social Studies

Coyote
and the

A Tale from Ayutla, Mexico

retold by Verna Aardema
illustrated by Petra Mathers

On a farm at the foot of a mountain, there once lived a little ewe lamb. Her master called her simply *Borreguita*, which means "little lamb."

One day Borreguita's master tied her to a stake in a field of red clover. The lamb was eating the lush plants when a coyote came along.

The coyote growled, "*Grrr*! Borreguita, I'm going to eat you!"

Borreguita bleated, "*Baa-a-a-a, baa-a-a-a*! Oh, Señor Coyote, I would not fill you up. I am as thin as a bean pod. When I have eaten all this clover, I shall be fat. You may eat me *then*."

Coyote looked at the skinny little lamb and the wide clover field. "*Está bien*. That is good," he said. "When you are fat, I shall come back."

After many days the coyote returned. He found the lamb grazing in a meadow. He growled, "*Grrr*! Borreguita, you are as plump as a tumbleweed. I'm going to eat you *now*!"

Borreguita bleated, *"Baa-a-a-a, baa-a-a-a!* Señor Coyote, I know something that tastes ever so much better than lamb!"

"What?" asked Coyote.

"Cheese!" cried Borreguita. "My master keeps a round of cheese on his table. He eats it on his tacos."

The coyote had never heard of cheese, and he was curious about it. "How can I get some of this cheese?" he asked.

Borreguita said, "There is a pond at the end of the pasture. Tonight, when the moon is high, meet me there. And I will show you how to get a cheese."

"Está bien," said Coyote. "I will be there."

That night, when the full moon was straight up in the sky, Borreguita and Coyote met at the edge of the pond.

There, glowing in the black water, was something that looked like a big, round cheese.

"Do you see it?" cried Borreguita. "Swim out and get it."

Coyote slipped into the water and paddled toward the cheese. He swam and swam, *shuh, shuh, shuh, shuh.* But the cheese stayed just so far ahead. Finally, he opened his mouth and lunged—WHOOOSH!

The image shattered in the splash!

Pond water rushed into Coyote's mouth. Coughing and spluttering, he turned and headed for the shore.

When he reached it, the little lamb was gone. She had tricked him! Coyote shook the water off his fur, *freh, freh, freh.*

Then he looked up at the big cheese in the sky and howled, "OWOOOOOAH!"

At dawn the next day Borreguita went to graze near a small overhanging ledge of rock on the side of the mountain. She knew that the coyote would be coming after her, and she had a plan.

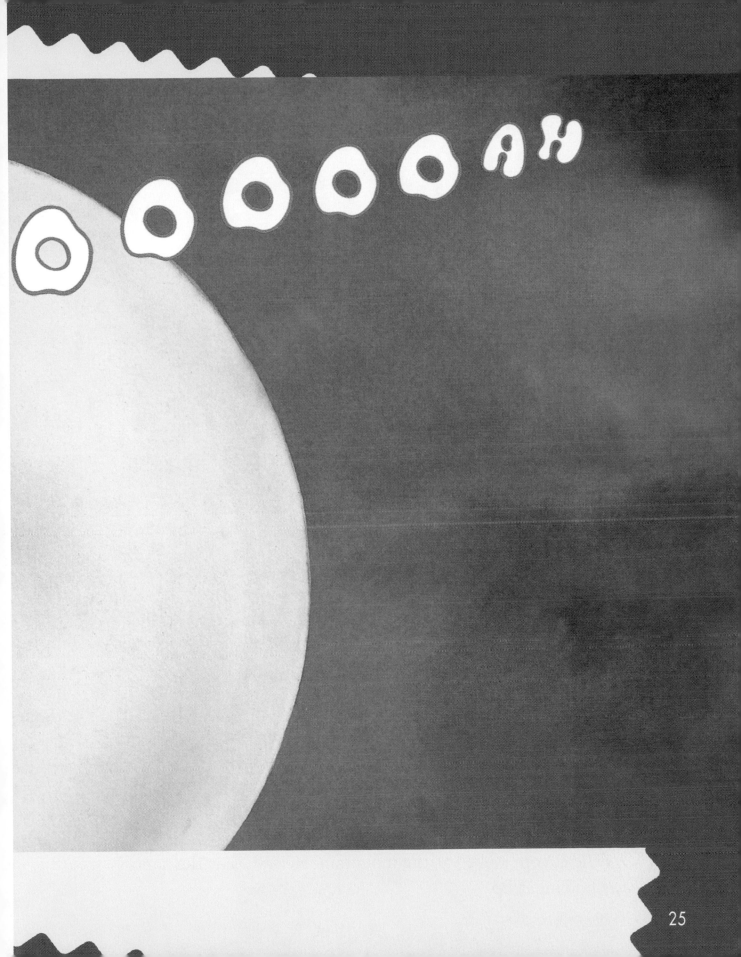

As the sun rose over the mountain, Borreguita saw the coyote coming. He was sniffing along, with his nose on some trail. She crawled under the ledge and lay on her back, bracing her feet against the top.

When the coyote found her, he growled, "*Grrr!* Borreguita, I see you under there. I'm going to pull you out and eat you!"

Borreguita bleated, "*Baa-a-a-a, baa-a-a-a!* Señor Coyote, you can't eat me *now*! I have to hold up this mountain. If I let go, it will come tumbling down."

The coyote looked at the mountain. He saw that the lamb was holding it up.

"You are strong," said Borreguita. "Will you hold it while I go for help?"

The coyote did not want the mountain to fall, so he crept under the ledge and put up his feet.

"Push hard," said Borreguita. "Do you have it now?"

"I have it," said Coyote. "But hurry back. This mountain is heavy."

Borreguita rolled out of the shallow cave and went leaping and running all the way back to the barnyard.

Coyote held up that rock until his legs ached and he was hungry and thirsty. At last he said, "Even if the mountain falls, I'm going to let go! I can't hold it any longer."

The coyote dragged himself out and covered his head with his paws. The mountain did not fall. Then he knew—the little lamb had fooled him again.

Coyote sat on his haunches and howled, "OWOOOOOAH!"

Early the next morning the coyote hid himself in a thicket in the lamb's pasture. When she drew near, he sprang out with a WOOF! And he said, "Borreguita, you will not escape this time! I'm going to eat you *now*!"

Borreguita bleated, *"Baa-a-a-a, baa-a-a-a!* Señor Coyote, I know I deserve to die. But grant me one kindness. Swallow me whole so that I won't have to suffer the biting and the chewing."

"Why should I make you comfortable while I eat you?" demanded the coyote. "Anyway, I couldn't swallow you all in one piece even if I wanted to."

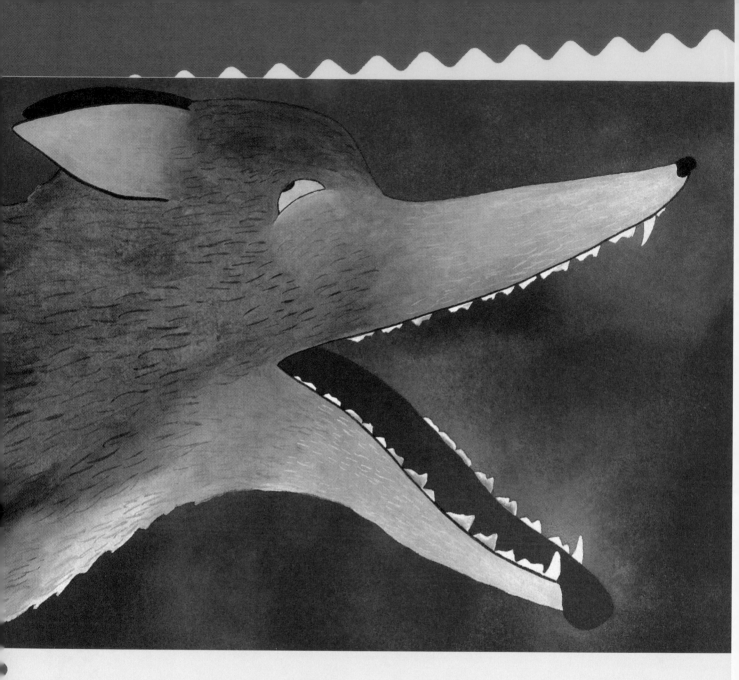

"Oh, yes, you could!" cried Borreguita. "Your mouth is so big, you could swallow a cougar. Open it wide, and I will run and dive right in."

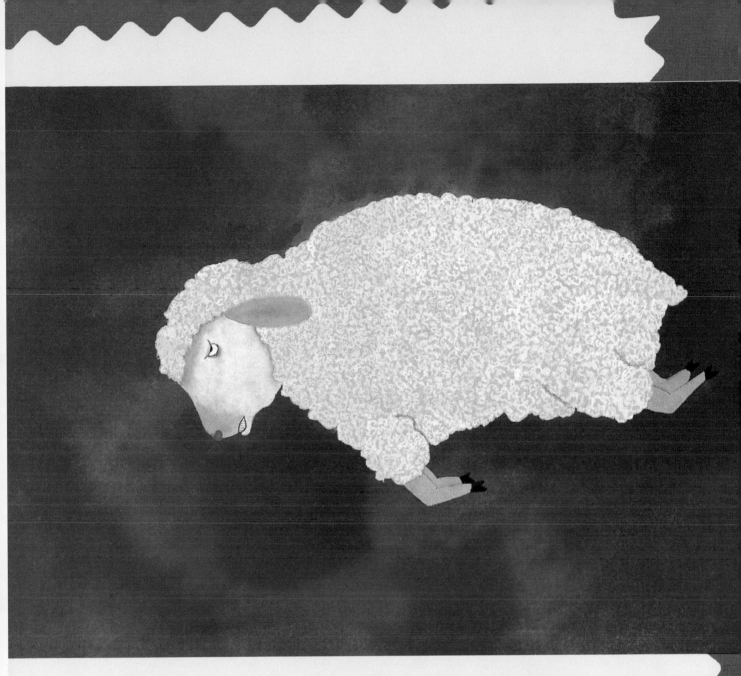

Coyote opened his mouth wide and braced his feet. Borreguita backed away. Then she put her head down and charged. BAM! She struck the inside of Coyote's mouth so hard she sent him rolling.

"OW, OW, OW!" howled the coyote as he picked himself up and ran away—his mouth feeling like one big toothache!

And from that day on, Borreguita frisked about on the farm at the foot of the mountain. And Coyote never bothered her again.

THE END
FIN

As a child, Verna Aardema loved to read. Her family often had a hard time tearing her away from the book she was reading at the time—even when she had to help out around the house!

When Verna was in the sixth grade, she wrote a poem that she was very proud of. As soon as Verna's mother read it, she knew her daughter would be a writer. From then on, Verna's mother encouraged her daughter whenever she could. Verna would run out the door right after dinner and go to a nearby swamp to think about the things she wanted to write. Soon, she was making up stories and telling them to the kids in her neighborhood.

"Writing is not easy but the rewards are great! When starry-eyed boys and girls tell me they want to be authors, I hug them for success."

Verna Aardema has now written more than twenty books for children, retelling popular folktales. Like most authors, she spends time revising her work. See the next page, which shows an early draft of "Borreguita and the Coyote."

Borreguita and the Coyote
A Tale from Ayutla
Mexico

On a farm at the foot of a mountain in Mexico, there once lived a little ewe lamb. Her master called her simply *Borreguita*, which means "little lamb."

One day Borreguita's master tied her to a stake in an alfalfa field. The lamb was eating the lush green plants when a coyote came along.

The coyote said, "Borreguita, I'm going to eat you!"

Borreguita bleated, "BA-A-A, BA-A-A! Oh, Señor Coyote, I would not fill you up. I am thin as a bean pod. When I have eaten all this alfalfa, I shall be fat. You may eat me then."

Coyote looked at the skinny little lamb and the wide alfalfa field. "*Está bien*. That is good," he said. "When you are fat, I shall come back."

After many days the coyote returned. He found the lamb grazing in a meadow. He said, "Borreguita, you are as plump as a tumbleweed. I'm going to eat you now!"

"Señor Coyote," cried Borreguita, "I know something that tastes ever so much better than lamb!"

"What?" asked Coyote.

"Cheese!" cried Borreguita. "My master keeps a round of cheese on his table. He eats it on his tacos."

The coyote had never heard of cheese, and he was curious about it. "How can I get some of this cheese?" he asked.

Borreguita said, "There is a pond at the end of the pasture. Tonight, when the moon is high, meet me there. And I will show you how to get a cheese."

"*Está bien*," said Coyote. "I will be there."

That night, when the full moon was straight up in the sky, Borreguita and Coyote met at the edge of the pond.

There, glowing in the black water, was something that looked like a big, round cheese.

"Do you see it?" cried Borreguita. "Swim out and get it."

Coyote slipped into the water and paddled toward the cheese. He swam and swam, but the cheese stayed just so far ahead. Finally, he opened his mouth and lunged—WHOOSH!

35

Response Corner

Postcards from Ayutla

Look in an atlas for a map of Mexico. Use the index to help you locate the city of Ayutla. Notice the landforms and bodies of water nearby. What would you see if you visited Ayutla? Write a postcard describing the area to your friends back home. On the front of your postcard, draw a scene that you might see in Ayutla.

Brains or Brawn?

Like "Borreguita and the Coyote," many other stories have one character who is weak but successful. With a classmate, make a list of story characters like Borreguita, who were more successful than a stronger character. For each character, write a sentence telling what qualities helped him or her to succeed.

The Moral of the Story...

Coyote finally learned his lesson after many troubles. Think about a lesson you learned the hard way. Then write a one-page short story with a moral, or lesson, at the end. Draw pictures to go with your story. You and your classmates may want to make a book of your stories.

What Do You Think?

▼ How does Borreguita outsmart Coyote?

▼ What is your favorite illustration in this story? Describe what it shows, and tell why you like it.

▼ Coyote is a character in many Native American and Mexican stories. What is he like in this story?

Award-Winning
Author and
Illustrator

BY GAIL GIBBONS

GRAY WOLF OR
TIMBER WOLF

It is a snowy moonlit night in the northern woods. An animal shakes the snow from its thick fur, throws its head back and joins its companions in a long howl. The animal is a wolf.

There are two different types of wolves. One is the gray wolf, or timber wolf. A gray wolf can have black, white, brown or gray fur depending on where it lives. Thirty-two different kinds of gray wolves have been identified. Some of them don't exist anymore.

RED WOLF

The other type of wolf is the red wolf. Red wolves aren't really red. Instead, they are the combination of black, gray and reddish brown. They are smaller and more slender than gray wolves. Only one of the three original different kinds of red wolves exists today. Very few of them live in the wild.

The first ancestors of wolves lived more than 50 million years ago. Over time, these creatures developed into wolves.

Wolves are members of the dog family, called Canidae. All dogs are related to wolves.

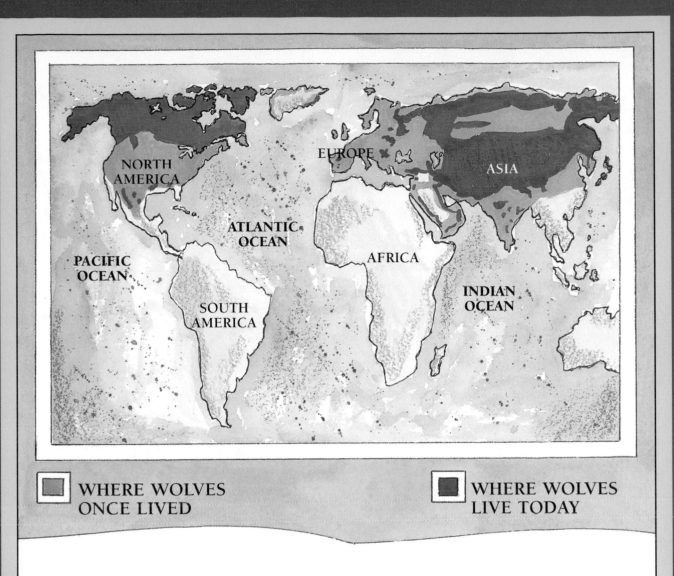

NORTH
AMERICA

EUROPE

ASIA

ATLANTIC
OCEAN

PACIFIC
OCEAN

AFRICA

SOUTH
AMERICA

INDIAN
OCEAN

WHERE WOLVES
ONCE LIVED

WHERE WOLVES
LIVE TODAY

A few hundred years ago, wolves lived all around the world.
People hunted them and also took over much of their territory.
There were fewer wolves and they moved away. Today most wolves
are found in the northern parts of the world.

Most male wolves weigh more than 100 pounds. The females
weigh less. Wolves are very strong and have long legs, a long tail,
and are covered with fur.

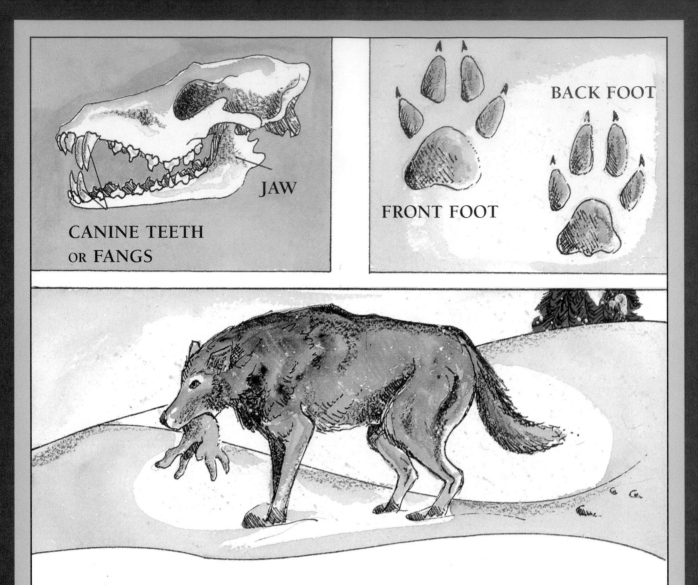

CANINE TEETH or FANGS

JAW

FRONT FOOT

BACK FOOT

Wolves are hunters. They are carnivores, which means they eat meat. They have strong jaws and forty-two teeth for tearing, chewing and grinding. Four of the teeth are called canine teeth, or fangs. Wolves use their canine teeth to grip an animal when they catch it.

Wolves have a keen sense of smell for sniffing out their prey. They can hear sounds from far away, too. When wolves roam, they leave big paw prints behind. Some tracks can be as large as a grownup's hand.

Gray wolves live in groups called packs. These packs can be made up of three to more than twenty wolves. It is believed that red wolves don't form packs. Wolf packs live and hunt in territories which can cover an area as big as 500 square miles. They mark the boundaries with their urine, which leaves a scent that warns other wolf packs to stay away. Each pack has adult males and females, and their pups.

The leader of a pack is called an alpha wolf. An alpha wolf is smart and strong. He will fight any wolf that tries to take over his pack. The alpha wolf is the tallest in the pack. When he looks the other wolves in the eye, they crouch down and tuck their tails between their hind legs. Sometimes they roll over and lick the alpha wolf's face, letting him know he's boss.

The members of a pack care for each other. They protect each other when other wolf packs try to invade their territory. They hunt and share their food together, too. The alpha wolf decides where and when to hunt. It would be difficult for a wolf to catch a big animal alone. Hunting in packs helps them survive.

Once they spot their prey, the chase begins. Wolves' legs are built for speed and running long distances. Often, an animal outruns them. Other times the prey tires and slows down.

The pack fans out in a circle around the animal. Then one wolf charges and attacks the animal. It hangs on tightly. Others attack.

Soon the fight is over. The hungry wolves can eat. Wolves hunt many different kinds of animals like moose, deer and caribou. They also hunt smaller animals such as rabbits, beavers and small rodents.

Wolves make different sounds to "talk" to each other. They whimper when they are excited or restless. A snarl means the wolf is being threatened. A short woof is a warning, and a bark means danger is near.

Wolves howl, too. The sound is eerie and sometimes seems sad. They howl to tell other packs to stay out of their territory. Often, it is the way they stay in touch with the others in their pack when they are separated. Sometimes they howl before a hunt.

Wolves communicate in other ways, too. They show their teeth when they are angry. When a wolf is scared, its ears go flat against its head. A wagging tail means the wolf is happy. If just the tip of the tail wags, it could be ready to attack.

Wolves often mate for life. Wolf pups are born in the spring. The alpha female is the only one of the females in a pack to give birth to a litter of pups. There can be three to fourteen pups. They only weigh about one pound at birth and cannot see or hear. They nuzzle up against their mother to drink her milk in the den where they live.

When the pups are about three weeks old, they are allowed out of their den to romp and play. The mother and some of the other wolves take turns babysitting while the rest of the pack is hunting. When the hunters return, the pups greet them. When they lick the wolves' jaws, the wolves bring up some of the food they have eaten and feed it to the pups. The pups are now old enough to eat meat.

At six months old the pups are almost as big as the adult wolves. They are strong enough and old enough to begin learning how to hunt. They join the pack as it roams in search of food.

For centuries people have been afraid of wolves. They thought wolves were their enemies. Scientists who study wolves are learning that wolves have been misunderstood. Wolves tend to live peacefully among themselves. They are shy and rarely attack people. When this happens, they have probably been threatened.

When wolves hunt, often the animals they kill are weak and sickly. The healthy and stronger animals survive. Wolves are not cruel. They are just very efficient hunters.

Occasionally wolves attack farm or ranch animals. This can make the farmers or ranchers want to kill them. Wolves are hunted for their fur, too.

Because wolves are in danger of extinction, some people realize they must be protected. Some scientists and people who work at zoos help wolves by raising them so they can be released into the wild. In many parts of the world laws have been passed making it illegal to hunt wolves.

By studying wolves in their natural surroundings and watching them for long periods of time, scientists have learned that wolves play an important part in the balance of our natural world. The old fears and myths about wolves are dying. Wolves deserve to live undisturbed.

If enough people care, there will be wild wolves for years to come, and the howling sounds these beautiful creatures make will still be heard.

MORE WAYS OF THE WOLVES

Wolves are the largest of the wild dogs, which include coyotes, foxes, and others.

Wolves have very few enemies. These enemies can be other packs of wolves, bears, and people.

Wolves usually trot or run in a way called loping. They are very fast runners. Some can run up to forty miles per hour.

A pack of howling wolves can be heard from as far away as ten miles.

When wolves hunt in snow, they walk in single file. They take turns making tracks for the others to walk in.

Wolves vary in size. The smallest kind in the world is the Arabian wolf. It is only about 32 inches long.

In North America there is no record of a healthy wolf ever attacking a person.

Some experts believe ancient people learned how to hunt by watching packs of wolves hunt.

Wolves are good swimmers but rarely follow prey into water during a chase.

In captivity, wolves have been known to live up to seventeen years. In the wild, life is much harder. Wolves usually live to be only nine to ten years old.

GAIL GIBBONS

Talks About Wolves

Our family lives out in the country in Vermont. When my daughter was about twelve, she saw a wolf as she was coming home from school. It startled her, and then it ran away. Actually, they both ran. My daughter ran into the house while the wolf ran into the woods.

Around the same time, I noticed several articles in the newspaper about wolves. One was about wolves in Alaska, and the other was about putting wolves back into the national forests. There are so many myths about wolves that I decided to write a book about them and find out the truth for myself.

When I write, I do the research for the book first. Also, it's very important for me to actually see what I'm writing about. For this book, I

spent time at the Bronx Zoo, where I observed wolves.

After I've done my research and written the book, I find an expert who can help me check my work. For me, a book takes about a year from the time I get an idea to the time I send it off to my editor. Usually, I'm working on several books at once. 🐾

Response

WRITE A STORY

THE REAL STORY

You read in the selection that there are many myths about wolves that are not true. Write a short story that helps show the truth about wolves. You might make the main character a wolf who is in danger. Help your reader see some good things about wolves.

WRITE AN AD

A WOLF'S FRIEND

Lawmakers and scientists are just some of the people who are trying to protect wolves. Study advertisements in a newspaper. Then write your own ad, asking for volunteers to help save wolves. Try to make people see that this project is important.

Corner

MAKE A POSTER

SAFETY IN THE WILD

Many people want to save wolves. Others, such as hikers and campers, may fear them. People in forest areas need to be very careful because wild animals can be dangerous. Make a poster of safety tips to help people be safe around wild animals.

WHAT DO YOU THINK?

■ How does Gail Gibbons feel about wolves? How do you know?

■ What else would you like to know about wolves? Where could you find that information?

■ Should animals always be allowed to roam wherever they want? Why or why not?

ART &
LITERATURE

In this theme, you have been reading about how animals survive in nature. How is this Chinese painting like the selections you have read? Why do you think the frog is watching the dragonflies?

The Detroit Institute of Arts;
Founders Society Purchase.

EARLY AUTUMN

by Qian Xuan

Qian Xuan painted this picture about seven hundred years ago.
Artists at that time used brushes dipped in different ink colors to
make their paintings. They spoke of "writing" a painting.

Wolf Island

by Celia Godkin

Outstanding Science Trade Book

Once there was an island. It was an island with trees and meadows, and many kinds of animals. There were mice, rabbits and deer, squirrels, foxes and several kinds of birds.

All the animals on the island depended on the plants and the other animals for their food and well-being. Some animals ate grass or other plants; some ate insects; some ate other animals. The island animals were healthy. There was plenty of food for all.

A family of wolves lived on the island, too, a male wolf, a female, and their five cubs.

One day the wolf cubs were playing on the beach while their mother and father slept. The cubs found a strange object at the edge of the water.

Wolf
Island

Celia Godkin

It was a log raft, nailed together with boards. The cubs had never seen anything like this before. They were very curious. They climbed onto it and sniffed about. Everything smelled different.

While the cubs were poking around, the raft began to drift slowly out into the lake. At first the cubs didn't notice anything wrong. Then, suddenly, there was nothing but water all around the raft.

The cubs were scared. They howled. The mother and father wolf heard the howling and came running down to the water's edge.

They couldn't turn the raft back, and the cubs were too scared to swim, so the adult wolves swam out to the raft and climbed aboard. The raft drifted slowly and steadily over to the mainland. Finally it came to rest on the shore and the wolf family scrambled onto dry land.

There were no longer wolves on the island.

Time passed. Spring grew into summer on the island, and summer into fall. The leaves turned red. Geese flew south, and squirrels stored up nuts for the winter.

Winter was mild that year, with little snow. The green plants were buried under a thin white layer. Deer dug through the snow to find food. They had enough to eat.

Next spring, many fawns were born.

There were now many deer on the island. They were eating large amounts of grass and leaves. The wolf family had kept the deer population down, because wolves eat deer for food. Without wolves to hunt the deer, there were now too many deer on the island for the amount of food available.

Spring grew into summer and summer into fall. More and more deer ate more and more grass and more and more leaves.

Rabbits had less to eat, because the deer were eating their food. There were not many baby bunnies born that year.

Foxes had less to eat, because there were fewer rabbits for them to hunt.

Mice had less to eat, because the deer had eaten the grass and grass seed. There were not many baby mice born that year.

Owls had less to eat, because there were fewer mice for them to hunt. Many animals on the island were hungry.

The first snow fell. Squirrels curled up in their holes, wrapped their tails around them for warmth, and went to sleep. The squirrels were lucky. They had collected a store of nuts for winter.

Other animals did not have winter stores. They had to find food in the snow. Winter is a hard time for animals, but this winter was harder than most. The snow was deep and the weather cold. Most of the plants had already been eaten during the summer and fall. Those few that remained were hard to find, buried deep under the snow.

Rabbits were hungry. Foxes were hungry. Mice were hungry. Owls were hungry. Even the deer were hungry. The whole island was hungry.

The owls flew over to the mainland, looking for mice. They flew over the wolf family walking along the mainland shore. The wolves were thin and hungry, too. They had not found a home, because there were other wolf families on the mainland. The other wolves did not want to share with them.

Snow fell for many weeks. The drifts became deeper and deeper. It was harder and harder for animals to find food. Animals grew weaker, and some began to die. The deer were so hungry they gnawed bark from the trees. Trees began to die.

Snow covered the island. The weather grew colder and colder. Ice began to form in the water around the island, and along the mainland coast. It grew thicker and thicker, spreading farther and farther out into the open water. One day there was ice all the way from the mainland to the island.

The wolf family crossed the ice and returned to their old home.

The wolves were hungry when they reached the island, and there were many weak and sick deer for them to eat. The wolves left the healthy deer alone.

Finally, spring came. The snow melted, and grass and leaves began to grow. The wolves remained in their island home, hunting deer. No longer would there be too many deer on the island. Grass and trees would grow again. Rabbits would find enough food. The mice would find enough food. There would be food for the foxes and owls. And there would be food for the deer. The island would have food enough for all.

Life on the island was back in balance.

Nature's Great Balancing Act

photograph by
Campbell Norsgaard

Outstanding
Science
Trade Book

IN OUR OWN BACKYARD

BY E. JAEDIKER NORSGAARD

Welcome to our backyard!

You won't find a tame grass carpet, but a large semi-wild wonderland that stretches from our house to the bordering woods. Some years ago we decided to let everything grow as it pleases. Now it's a community where many of our fellow creatures are at home. On a summer day, grasshoppers will jump away from your footsteps. You'll see bees buzzing around raspberry bushes, butterflies landing on wildflowers, birds feeding insects to their young. There are chipmunks and a family of bold raccoons. Deer venture out of the woods to nibble hedges and shrubs.

photograph by Campbell Norsgaard

All creatures in the animal kingdom depend on plants and on each other for survival, one feeding on another. They are all parts of a gigantic puzzle in which the pieces fit together but, like a kaleidoscope, are forever changing. You are a mammal, and you are a part of that puzzle too, though you are quite different from other mammals and from birds, reptiles, amphibians, and insects. All living things are members of nature's great balancing act. You can see how this works right here in our own backyard.

Nature's great balancing act depends on food chains. All food chains begin with plants. Plants are able to make their own food, using energy from the sun, and they pass that energy on to animals that eat them. Plants are the basis of all the food and energy that you and other animals use.

When an animal eats a plant or eats another animal, it becomes part of a food chain. In our backyard, as well as everywhere else, all food chains begin with plant-eaters (herbivores) and usually end with a meat-eater (carnivore). Food chains can be short or as long as five or six links. If you eat

Like many mammals, this red fox eats plants and animals.

an apple, that is a two-link food chain. If you eat meat from a sheep or cow that has eaten plants, that is a three-link food chain. You are at the top of those food chains.

Here in the backyard, one food chain might begin with a moth sipping nectar from a flower. The moth is caught by a sparrow and fed to its young in the nest in our hedge. The young bird might be taken from its nest and eaten by a raccoon. The raccoon is at the top of this food chain. There are no predators[1] in the backyard to eat the raccoon.

---

[1] **predators**: animals that live by eating other animals

ENERGY
comes from the sun.

PLANT
uses the
sun's energy.

RACCOON
eats sparrows.

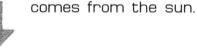

SPARROWS
eat moth.

MOTH
sips nectar
from plant.

Another food chain might start with a fly feeding on decaying vegetation[2] in the backyard. The fly is caught and eaten by a spider. The spider is eaten by a toad, which is eaten by a fox.

First links in any food chain are usually the smallest but most abundant plants and animals. Microscopic green algae and other plant plankton[3] float in the ponds, lakes, and seas. They are eaten in great quantities by water insects and small crustaceans,[4] which are eaten by small fishes, which are, in turn, eaten by larger fishes that may end up on your dinner table.

Each time an animal eats a plant or one animal eats another, a tiny bit of the sun's energy is passed along the food chain. Each animal uses some of that energy and passes along what is left. Amazingly, the used energy is not destroyed, only changed into other forms or passed into the atmosphere.[5]

BALANCING POPULATIONS

Animal populations are kept in balance by the amount of food available and by predators in the food chain. Take mice, for instance. You can't really catch sight of them scurrying through the tall grass in the backyard, eating seeds. They move quickly to avoid enemies. During a summer of heavy rainfall and lush vegetation, the mouse population

---

[2] **decaying vegetation**: rotting plants
[3] **algae and plant plankton**: simple plants that float or drift in the water

[4] **crustaceans**: animals with a tough shell that live in water, like lobsters and crabs
[5] **atmosphere**: the air around the earth

This long-eared owl helps keep the mouse population in balance.

increases, providing more food for hawks and owls and other mouse-eaters. When less food is available, mice tend to raise fewer young. This affects the numbers of hawks and owls also. If the insect and rodent populations decrease,[6] owls and hawks raise fewer young or find better territory or else starve. A balance of numbers is maintained.

Some farmers shoot hawks and owls, believing that they kill a few chickens. But without these predators, rabbits and mice overpopulate and spread into cultivated fields to eat corn, wheat, oats, rye, barley, rice, and sugar cane—the grasses which are first links in human food chains. This is what happens when we upset a balanced community.

[6] **decrease:** to go down in size or number

71

FEATHERED KEEPERS

Birds are a great help in keeping the numbers of insects in balance.

The friendly chickadees are greeting us from the lilac bushes, with their cheerful call . . . dee-dee-dee . . . between dashes to the feeder for sunflower seeds, or excursions into the brush for caterpillars and other insects and spiders.

A couple of barn swallows are catching winged insects to feed their babies in a mud-and-straw nest on a high beam in our garden tool shed.

These newly hatched barn swallows rely on their parents for food.

A pair of cardinals is swooping down on grasshoppers. I can't help hoping that no snake or owl raids their nest in the hedge, but that's a possibility.

The tiny house wren parents are tireless hunters, making continuous trips from dawn until dark to satisfy the high-pitched hunger cries of their babies in the nest box near our kitchen window. A young bird may eat its weight in insects every day!

In the spring, we watch the birds compete for inchworms, hopping from twig to twig, picking the leaves clean.

We saw the female Baltimore oriole peel dried fibers off last year's tall dogbane plant with her beak and fly high up in the oak tree to weave them into her nest. She and the male who courted and won her fed their nestlings with soft parts of insects, and themselves ate caterpillars, beetles, wasps,

This young blue jay is not yet ready to hunt for its own food.

grasshoppers, and ants.

Young blue jays with innocent faces and fresh white and blue feathers follow their parents around, fluttering their wings to be fed, although they've grown as large as the adults.

Birds are a joy to watch as they go about their business, protecting the plants in our backyards and gardens from an oversupply of leaf-eating insects.

Too many grasshoppers can be harmful to a garden.

MAMMALS

A family of deer often comes out of the small woods bordering our backyard and browses among the plants. When we go outside, they stop and stare at us with wide eyes, then turn and leap gracefully away, wiggling their white tails.

In winter, they walk through the snow up to the house itself to nibble hedges and shrubs. Deer can double their numbers in a single year. Long ago, their populations were kept in check mainly by cougars (mountain lions) that leaped on them from low tree limbs. And by packs of wolves, and by native American Indians who hunted them for food, buckskins, and doeskins. Today, without predators except man in many places, deer sometimes eat every leaf and bud in their range, and some starve in winter.

Without predators, these deer can upset the balance of nature.

The lively little chipmunks have found an easy way to make a living. Besides collecting wild plant seeds, one is sitting near the bird feeder, stuffing so many fallen sunflower seeds into his mouth that the pouches in his cheeks puff up like small balloons. He races to his underground nest to store them away and is soon back for more, running quickly to avoid hawks and other predators.

Chipmunks store nuts and seeds for the cold winter months ahead.

A red fox sometimes walks stealthily into our backyard at sunset, hunting mice and birds. The chipmunks dart into their burrows where they're safe from the fox, but not from weasels.

As we wait for more furry visitors, the evening air is filled with scraping sounds of katydids calling their own names, and the high jingle bell chorus of snowy tree crickets. They feed on the foliage[7] in which they hide, daring to advertise for mates at night when the birds that prey on them are asleep.

---

[7] **foliage**: the leaves on trees and plants

 Katydids hide from their enemies by blending in with leaves and branches.

A family of raccoons and an opossum make trails through the backyard, stopping to munch berries. This is part of their regular rounds as they seek out mice, lizards, grasshoppers, and crickets, and grub in the mud for frogs.

Opossums eat many different kinds of animals.

Frogs live in the mud and can catch flying insects with their long tongues.

In case they're still hungry, the raccoons are bold enough to look in our kitchen window or tap on the door and invite themselves in for a snack. The opossum, who eats almost anything, gets in on the act. After all, humans have taken over much of their territory.

This bold raccoon is looking for a snack in an unusual place!

A bug sat in a silver flower
Thinking silver thoughts.
A bigger bug out for a walk
Climbed up that silver flower stalk
And snapped the small bug down his jaws
Without a pause
Without a care
For all the bug's small silver thoughts.
It isn't right
It isn't fair
That big bug ate that little bug
Because that little bug was there.

He also ate his underwear.

WRITE A NEWS STORY

THIS JUST IN...

Write a television news story for the Backyard News Network (BNN). Give the latest facts on the crime described in "A Bug Sat in a Silver Flower." Has the big bug been caught? Where was he last seen? Read your bulletin to your classmates.

WRITE MENUS

PYRAMIDS ARE NOT JUST IN EGYPT

Do you know where to find a food pyramid? It's not a place you visit. It's a healthful eating plan. Study the food pyramid shown on a food label. Then use the pyramid to help you write healthful menus for breakfast, lunch, and dinner for one week. Share your menus with your family or classmates.

IN YOUR OWN SCHOOLYARD

Take a walk outside around your school with your teacher and classmates. Take notes on the different plants and animals you see. With classmates, create a mural showing the food chain in your area. Display the mural in class.

CORNER

WHAT DO YOU THINK?

🐾 How do different kinds of animals "balance" each other?

🐾 Would you like to have a backyard like the one you read about? Why or why not?

🐾 What would happen if there were no birds in the backyard? How do you know?

ALL EYES ON

by
Michael J. Rosen

illustrated by
Tom Leonard

THE POND

Here and there
around this pond,
countless eyes watch
what goes on.
Listen. They're
all calling you:
Come closer, look!
Come see my view.

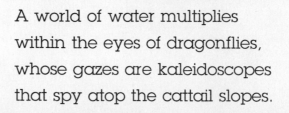

A world of water multiplies
within the eyes of dragonflies,
whose gazes are kaleidoscopes
that spy atop the cattail slopes.

The snapping turtle sometimes sees
the muddy deep, sometimes the trees,
and sometimes nothing but inside
the painted shell where it can hide.

From where the spider always clings
the view is largely tangled things
dangling in the crisscrossed strands
that weave the windows where it stands.

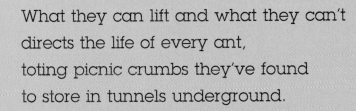

What they can lift and what they can't
directs the life of every ant,
toting picnic crumbs they've found
to store in tunnels underground.

The snail sees simply what it's on
as it glides up a stalk or frond.
Where next? The snail can still decide
as it glides down the other side.

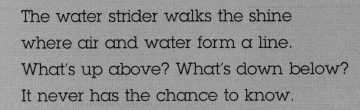

The water strider walks the shine
where air and water form a line.
What's up above? What's down below?
It never has the chance to know.

With echoes bouncing through the night,
the bat can see without its sight.
Soundless shadows, hidden prey—
a bat may swoop and snatch away.

To what's ahead, the crawdad's blind.
It only sees what's left behind.
Whooshing backward by its tail,
the crawdad leaves a cloudy trail.

Peering toward the breezy air
where clouds are what the branches bear,
the bluegill watches at the brink
the flitting things it hopes will sink.

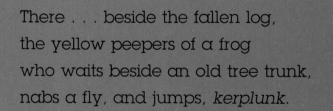

There . . . beside the fallen log,
the yellow peepers of a frog
who waits beside an old tree trunk,
nabs a fly, and jumps, *kerplunk*.

Paddling through the cattail shoots,
lily pads and toppled roots,
a mallard dips and dives and dunks
to munch upon the duckweed clumps.

Chittering swallows skitter so fast
and skim the waves as they soar past,
keeping an eye on all that's afloat—
a branch, a beetle, an anchored boat.

The pond itself, seen from the sky,
appears to be a giant's eye.
What's it watching, staring back?
A storm? The clouds? The zodiac?

If you were here, what would you spy
with your peculiar human eye?
Shhh. Come closer. What's your view?
All the creatures watch for you.

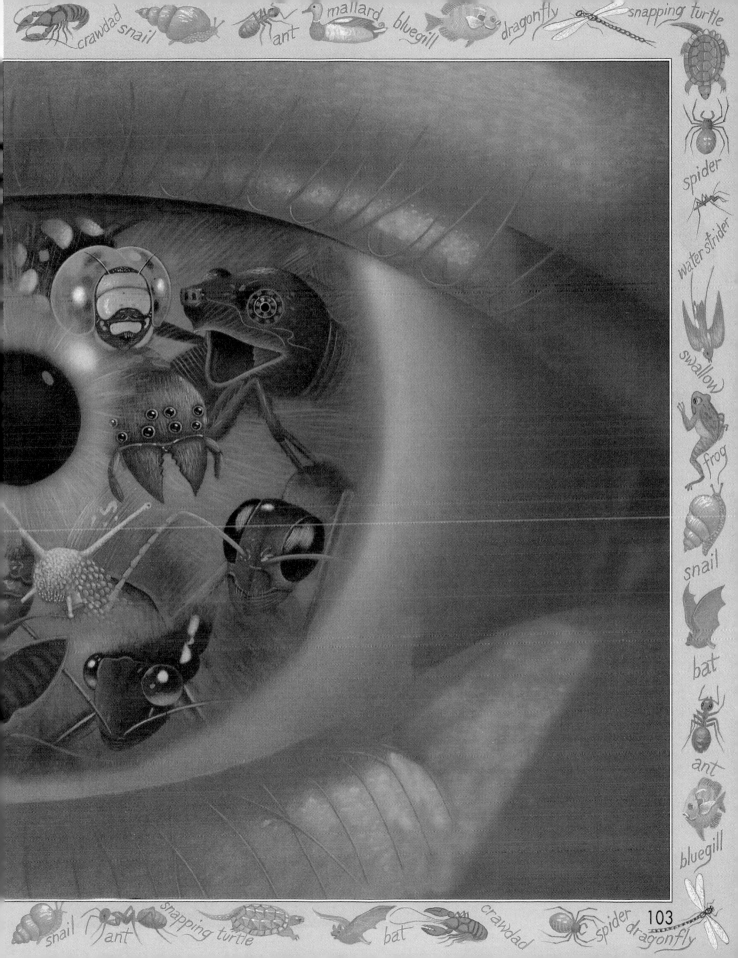

spider

water strider

swallow

frog

snail

bat

ant

bluegill

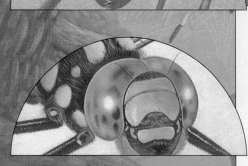

Meet the Illustrator . . .
Tom Leonard

Ilene Cooper talked to the illustrator of *All Eyes on the Pond*.

Ilene Cooper: *A book like this must take a lot of research.*

Tom Leonard: Yes. I spent about four months in libraries, looking at pictures. I took photographs at ponds and used them when I drew the plants and animals.

Cooper: *How did you decide on the way you would draw the illustrations for this book?*

Leonard: The title is *All Eyes on the Pond*, so I decided that eyes should be an important part of the book. I added a big eye above each word box. Then I added a curve to the box so that it was the shape of a human eye.

Cooper: *How did you get started drawing?*

Leonard: I was a cartoonist when I was young. After graduating from art school, I worked for newspapers and textbooks, and now I'm illustrating children's books. This is only my second one.

Michael J. Rosen

Ilene Cooper, an author herself, talked to the author of *All Eyes on the Pond.*

Ilene Cooper: *This book is about a different way of seeing, isn't it?*

Michael Rosen: Yes. Some people think it's about pond life, but it is really about how different creatures see the same thing. When I visit schools, I often ask children, "What does your pet see that you don't see?" I like changing places, thinking as some other person or creature.

Cooper: *Although you didn't illustrate this book, you are also an illustrator. Did you do a lot of writing and drawing as a child?*

Rosen: I remember I drew monsters. I didn't draw from real life—I didn't even know you could do that. All of my drawings came from my imagination.

Cooper: *Did you know that writing and illustrating were going to be your career?*

Rosen: No, I was going to be a doctor. But I met another writer, and I learned that writing could be more than a hobby—it could be a world that you both invent and live within.

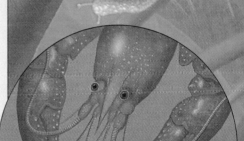

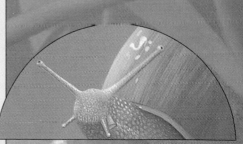

RESPONSE

WRITE A POEM

A Bug's-Eye View

Pond insects see the world in their own ways. How do insects in other environments see things? Pick a common insect that lives in a forest, field, desert, or swamp. Write a poem about how it sees its environment.

DRAW SKETCHES

A Nature Study

Find a quiet spot where you can observe a pet or another animal. Bring a sketch pad and a pencil or charcoal and draw several sketches of the animal. Choose your favorite sketch, and add color with paint or markers to create the finished picture. Then write one or two sentences telling what you learned about the animal.

frog water strider swallow crawdad spider mallard snail

ant bat snail swallow dragonfly bluegill mallard

snapping turtle water strider ant crawdad snail bluegill mallard

CORNER

PREPARE A REPORT

All About Eyesight

Animals see differently because their eyes are built differently. How are human eyes built? Work with a partner to prepare a short oral report about human eyes. Use pictures, charts, and other aids to make your report more interesting.

What Do You Think?

- Why do the different animals who live near the pond see different things?

- Which pond animal is your favorite? Why?

- What would you *hear* if you visited a pond? Describe the sounds some of the animals might make.

spider
water strider
swallow
frog
snail
bat
ant
bluegill

crawdad snail ant mallard bluegill dragonfly

snail ant snapping turtle bat crawdad spider dragonfly

THEME WRAP-UP

All living things—wild and tame, predators and prey—are part of the balance of nature. How is this fact shown in the selection "Wolves"? How is it shown in "Nature's Great Balancing Act"?

Understanding how animals live is important. What did you think of wolves before you read these stories, and what do you think of them now? Have you changed your mind about wolves? Explain your answer.

ACTIVITY CORNER

Choose an animal that must eat other animals to live. Read about the animal in an encyclopedia or a nonfiction book. Then write a short report about the animal's habits. Tell where it lives, what it eats, how it sleeps, and any other facts you find interesting.

Traveling to New Communities

Have you or members of your family ever lived in a different place? It's not always easy to move to a new community. But, as you will learn from the stories in this theme, new places can be exciting and interesting, too.

Traveling to New Communities

.CONTENTS.

Bookshelf

Dandelions
by Eve Bunting

When Zoe realizes that her mother misses the city she grew up in, she does something to make her mother feel more at home on the prairie.

Teachers' Choice

Signatures Library

DANDELIONS

Written by
EVE BUNTING

Illustrated by
GREG SHED

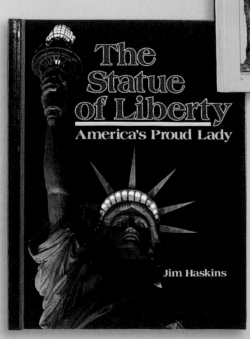

The Statue of Liberty
by Jim Haskins

America's "proud lady" has greeted countless immigrants with the promise of freedom.

Award-Winning Author

Signatures Library

Halmoni and the Picnic
by Sook Nyul Choi

Yunmi's third-grade class helps her grandmother feel comfortable in the United States.

Back Home
by Gloria Jean Pinkney

A city girl from the North learns about farm life in the South when she visits her mother's relatives.

ALA Notable Book; Notable Trade Book in Social Studies; Award-Winning Illustrator

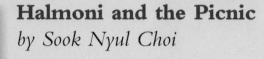

Amber Brown Goes Fourth
by Paula Danziger

Amber's best friend has moved. Who will help her face fourth grade?

Award-Winning Author

My
Great-Aunt
ARIZO

MY GREAT-AUNT
ARIZONA

BY
GLORIA HOUSTON · SUSAN CONDIE LAMB

NA

written by
Gloria Houston
illustrated by
Susan Condie Lamb

My great-aunt Arizona was born in a log cabin her papa built in the meadow on Henson Creek in the Blue Ridge Mountains. When she was born, the mailman rode across the bridge on his big bay horse with a letter.

The letter was from her brother, Galen, who was in the cavalry, far away in the West. The letter said, "If the baby is a girl, please name her Arizona, and she will be beautiful, like this land."

Arizona was a very tall little girl. She wore her long brown hair in braids. She wore long full dresses, and a pretty white apron. She wore high-button shoes, and many petticoats, too. Arizona liked to grow flowers.

She liked to read, and sing, and square dance to the music of the fiddler on Saturday night.

Arizona had a little brother, Jim. They played together on the farm. In summer they went barefoot and caught tadpoles in the creek.

In the fall they climbed the mountains searching for galax and ginseng roots.

In the winter they made snow cream with sugar, snow, and sweet cream from Mama's cows. When spring came, they helped Papa tap the maple trees and catch the sap in buckets. Then they made maple syrup and maple-sugar candy.

Arizona and her brother Jim walked up the road that wound by the creek to the one-room school. All the students in all the grades were there, together in one room. All the students read their lessons aloud at the same time. They made a great deal of noise, so the room was called a blab school.

The students carried their lunches in lard buckets made of tin. They brought ham and biscuits. Sometimes they had fried apple pie. They drank cool water from the spring at the bottom of the hill. At recess they played games like tag and William Matrimmatoe.

When Arizona had read all the books at the one-room school, she crossed the mountains to the school in another village, a village called Wing. It was so far away that she rode her papa's mule. Sometimes she rode the mule through the snow.

When Arizona's mother died, Arizona had to leave school and stay home to care for Papa and her brother Jim. But she still loved to read—and dream about the faraway places she would visit one day. So she read and she dreamed, and she took care of Papa and Jim.

Then one day Papa brought home a new wife. Arizona could go away to school, where she could learn to be a teacher. Aunt Suzie invited Arizona to live at her house and help with the chores. Aunt Suzie made her work very hard. But at night Arizona could study—and dream of all the faraway places she would visit one day.

Finally, Arizona returned to her home on Henson Creek. She was a teacher at last.

She taught in the one-room school where she and Jim had sat. She made new chalkboards out of lumber from Papa's sawmill, and covered them with polish made for shoes. She still wore long full dresses and a pretty white apron. She wore high-button shoes and many petticoats, too. She grew flowers in every window. She taught students about words and numbers and the faraway places they would visit someday.

"Have you been there?" the students asked.

"Only in my mind," she answered. "But someday you will go."

Arizona married the carpenter who helped
build the new Riverside School down where
Henson Creek joins the river. So Miss Arizona
became Mrs. Hughes, and for the rest of her
days she taught fourth-grade students who
called her "Miz Shoes."

And when her daughter was born,
Miz Shoes brought the baby to
school, to the sunny room where
flowers grew in every window.

Every year Arizona had a Christmas tree growing in a pot. The girls and boys made paper decorations to brighten up the tree. Then they planted their tree at the edge of the school yard, year after year, until the entire playground was lined with living Christmas trees, like soldiers guarding the room where Arizona taught, with her long gray braids wound 'round her head, with her long full dress, and pretty white apron, with her high-button shoes, and many petticoats, too.

The boys and girls who were students in her class had boys and girls who were students in her class. And they had boys and girls who were students in her class.

For fifty-seven years my great-aunt Arizona hugged her students. She hugged them when their work was good, and she hugged them when it was not. She taught them words and numbers, and about the faraway places they would visit someday.

"Have you been there?" the students asked.

"Only in my mind," she answered. "But someday you will go."

My great-aunt Arizona taught my dad, Jim's only son. And she taught my brother and me in the fourth grade. With her soft white braids wound 'round her head, she taught us about faraway places we would visit someday.

My great-aunt Arizona died on her ninety-third birthday. But she goes with me in my mind—A very tall lady, in a long full dress, and a pretty white apron, with her high-button shoes, and her many petticoats, too. She's always there, in a sunny room with many flowers in every window, and a hug for me every day.

She never did go to the faraway places she taught us about. But my great-aunt Arizona travels with me and with those of us whose lives she touched. . . .

She goes with us in our minds.

Gloria Houston

Gloria Houston, like her great-aunt Arizona, loves teaching. For fifteen years, she taught students in elementary school through high school. She now teaches writing and children's literature to college students in Tampa, Florida.

Gloria Houston says about her great-aunt, "She truly lives on in what she gave to her students, including me. I have traveled because she made the places in my geography book seem so real. Most important, she made each student feel special. Years later, each member of her class still thinks he or she was Aunt Arizona's pet."

Susan Condie Lamb

Susan Condie Lamb is a full-time artist who has illustrated many children's books. She has also designed sets and costumes for plays. She found that experience a big help as she drew pictures for *My Great-Aunt Arizona*.

Susan Condie Lamb grew up in Connecticut. Although she lived in New York City for a while, today she's back in Connecticut. She lives with her husband and her son, Charlie.

RESPONSE CORNER

A Note of Thanks

Arizona Hughes was an important adult in many children's lives. Choose an important adult in your life. Write a thank-you note telling that person why he or she is special to you.

The Little Red Schoolhouse

Work with a group to turn a corner of your classroom into a model of a one-room school. Use boxes and other materials to make the desks, the stove, and other furniture. Give a tour to your classmates. Explain how this school is different from your own school.

Wish You Were Here

Suppose Great-Aunt Arizona really had traveled to faraway places. Write one or two postcards that she might have sent to her students. Share the postcards with a partner.

What Do You Think?

- What kind of person was Arizona? How do you know?

- If you could go back to Arizona's time, what would you like to see and do?

- How might Arizona's life be different if she were living today? Explain your answer.

Grandfather's Journey

Caldecott Medal
ALA Notable Book
Teachers' Choice

written and illustrated
by Allen Say

My grandfather was a
young man when he left his
home in Japan and went to
see the world.

THE ISLANDS OF

He wore European clothes for the first time and began his
journey on a steamship. The Pacific Ocean astonished him.

For three weeks he did not see land. When land finally appeared it was the New World.

He explored North America by train and riverboat, and often walked for days on end.

Deserts with rocks like enormous sculptures amazed him.

The endless farm fields reminded him of the ocean he had crossed.

Huge cities of factories and tall buildings bewildered and yet
excited him.

He marveled at the towering mountains and rivers as clear as the sky.

He met many people along the way. He shook hands with black men and white men, with yellow men and red men.

The more he traveled, the more he longed to see new places, and never thought of returning home.

Of all the places he visited, he liked California best. He loved the strong sunlight there, the Sierra Mountains, the lonely seacoast.

After a time, he returned to his village in Japan to marry his
childhood sweetheart. Then he brought his bride to the new
country.

They made their home by the San Francisco Bay and had a baby girl.

As his daughter grew, my grandfather began to think about his own childhood. He thought about his old friends.

He remembered the mountains and rivers of his home. He surrounded himself with songbirds, but he could not forget.

Finally, when his daughter was nearly grown, he could wait no more. He took his family and returned to his homeland.

Once again he saw the mountains and rivers of his childhood.
They were just as he had remembered them.

Once again he exchanged stories and laughed with his old friends.

But the village was not a place for a daughter from San Francisco.
So my grandfather bought a house in a large city nearby.

There, the young woman fell in love, married, and sometime later I was born.

When I was a small boy, my favorite weekend was a visit to my grandfather's house. He told me many stories about California.

He raised warblers and silvereyes, but he could not forget the mountains and rivers of California. So he planned a trip.

But a war began. Bombs fell from the sky and scattered our lives like leaves in a storm.

When the war ended, there was nothing left of the city and of
the house where my grandparents had lived.

So they returned to the village where they had been children.
But my grandfather never kept another songbird.

The last time I saw him, my grandfather said that he longed to see California one more time. He never did.

And when I was nearly grown, I left home and went to see California for myself.

After a time, I came to love the land my grandfather had loved, and I stayed on and on until I had a daughter of my own.

But I also miss the mountains and rivers of my childhood. I miss my old friends. So I return now and then, when I can not still the longing in my heart.

The funny thing is, the moment I am in one country, I am homesick for the other.

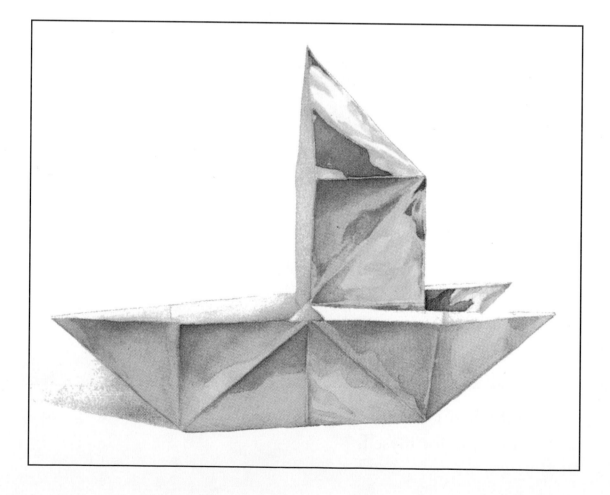

I think I know my grandfather now.
I miss him very much.

ALLEN SAY

Allen Say is one of America's most successful writers and illustrators of children's books. He spent two years creating *Grandfather's Journey.* After it was published in 1993, it won many of the highest honors in children's literature, including the Caldecott Medal. Allen Say's earlier books, including *El Chino, Tree of Cranes,* and *A River Dream,* have also won important awards.

Grandfather's Journey is fiction, but it is based on real life. Allen's grandfather truly was a world traveler, and he especially loved steamships. After traveling around the world, he lived in California for many years and then returned to Japan.

Allen was born in Yokohama, Japan. He began to draw even before he could walk. As a small child, Allen drew on walls, doors, and anything else he could reach. When he was twelve years old, he was thrilled to study art with a famous cartoonist in Japan.

At age sixteen, Allen Say moved to the United States. He found himself suddenly alone in a country he knew little about. He did not speak a word of English, and he felt out of place in his new school. It was a difficult time in Allen's life. He shows how he felt at that time in the painting on page 157. He says, "My favorite painting in *Grandfather's Journey* is the picture of myself, standing in the sun-drenched, empty parking lot. I love that painting."

Before Allen Say began making his living by painting, he worked as a photographer. If you look closely at the paintings in *Grandfather's Journey*, you might think they are a little like old-fashioned photographs. The people seem to be looking right at you, as if they are posing for a camera.

Allen Say has learned how to capture the feelings of his characters in his art. By sharing *Grandfather's Journey* with us, he is sharing the feelings of many immigrants to America. The next time you meet someone who has just moved to the United States, remember *Grandfather's Journey*. Remember how Allen Say must have felt as he stood in that empty parking lot.

THAT MOUNTAIN FAR AWAY

A TRADITIONAL TEWA POEM

My home over there, my home over there,

My home over there, now I remember it!

And when I see that mountain far away,

Why, then I weep. Alas! What can I do? . . .

My home over there, now I remember it.

TRAVEL

EDNA ST. VINCENT MILLAY

The railroad track is miles away,
   And the day is loud with voices speaking,
Yet there isn't a train goes by all day
   But I hear its whistles shrieking.

All night there isn't a train goes by,
   Though the night is still for sleep and dreaming
But I see its cinders red on the sky
   And hear its engine steaming.

My heart is warm with the friends I make,
   And better friends I'll not be knowing,
Yet there isn't a train I wouldn't take,
   No matter where it's going.

Train from Durango to Silverton, Colorado   *Photograph by David Herman*

Response

The Peaceful Pacific

Grandfather crossed the Pacific Ocean when he traveled from Japan to California. Look up the Pacific Ocean in an encyclopedia. Draw a map that shows the larger islands between Japan and the United States. On your map, write five interesting facts about the Pacific Ocean.

What's in Style?

When he lived in America, Grandfather wore Western-style clothing. In Japan, he wore a traditional kimono. Did your ancestors wear a special kind of clothing? If you can, bring that clothing to class and model it. Or bring in a photograph that shows it. How is the special clothing different from the clothing you wear today?

Corner

Far, Far Away

Allen Say's grandfather and the poet who wrote "Travel" liked to visit new places. Have you seen pictures in a magazine of a place that you would like to visit? Make a travel brochure of that place. Include photographs or magazine pictures.

What Do You Think?

- How is the grandson in the story like his grandfather?

- Which of the paintings from this story is your favorite? Explain why you like it.

- Think about somewhere far away that you would like to visit someday. How would you get there? What might you see?

165

The Lotus Seed

by Sherry Garland

illustrated by Tatsuro Kiuchi

HOA SEN

Trong đầm gì đẹp bằng sen.
Lá xanh, bông trắng lại chen nhị vàng.
Nhị vàng, bông trắng, lá xanh,
Gần bùn mà chẳng hôi tanh mùi bùn.

—Vô danh

THE LOTUS FLOWER

Nothing that grows in a pond
Surpasses the beauty of the lotus flower,
With its green leaves and silky yellow styles
Amidst milky white petals.
Though mired in mud, its silky yellow styles,
Its milky white petals and green leaves
Do not smell of mud.

— Anonymous
(translation of poem by Dinh D. Vu)

*M*y grandmother saw
the emperor cry
the day he lost
his golden dragon throne.

She wanted something
to remember him by,
so she snuck down
to the silent palace,
near the River of Perfumes,
and plucked a seed
from a lotus pod
that rattled
in the Imperial garden.

She hid the seed
in a special place
under the family altar,
wrapped in a piece of silk
from the *ao dai*
she wore that day.
Whenever she felt sad
or lonely,
she took out the seed
and thought of the
brave young emperor.

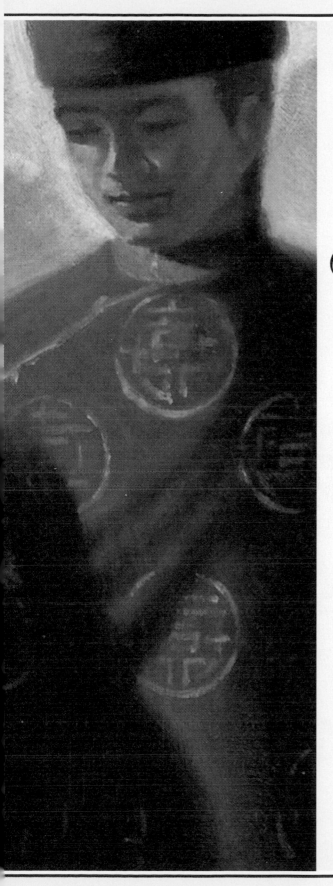

$\mathcal{A}$nd when she married
a young man
chosen by her parents,
she carried the seed
inside her pocket
for good luck, long life,
and many children.
When her husband
marched off to war,
she raised her
children alone.

One day bombs fell
all around,
and soldiers
clamored door to door.
She took the time
to grab the seed,
but left her mother-of-pearl
hair combs lying
on the floor.

One terrible day
her family scrambled
into a crowded boat
and set out
on a stormy sea.
Bà watched the mountains
and the waving palms
slowly fade away.
She held the seed
in her shaking fingers
and silently said good-bye.

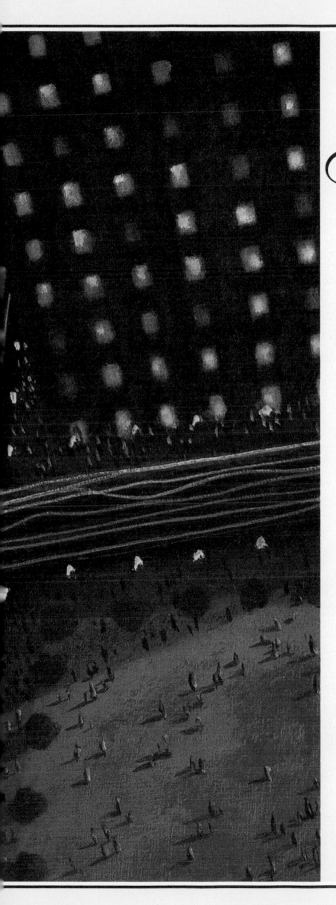

She arrived in a
strange new land
with blinking lights
and speeding cars
and towering buildings
that scraped the sky
and a language
she didn't understand.

She worked many years,
day and night,
and so did her children
and her sisters
and her cousins, too,
living together
in one big house.

*L*ast summer
my little brother
found the special seed
and asked questions
again and again.
He'd never seen a lotus bloom
or an emperor
on a golden dragon throne.

So one night
he stole the seed
from beneath the family altar
and planted it
in a pool of mud
somewhere near Bà's
onion patch.

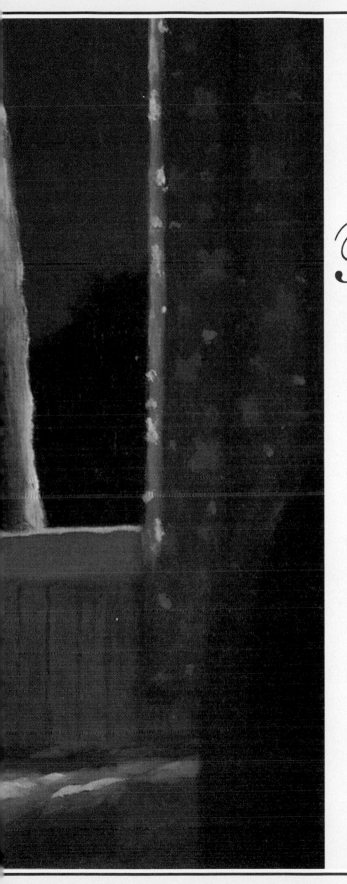

Bà cried and cried
when she found out
the seed was gone.
She didn't eat,
she didn't sleep,
and my silly brother
forgot what spot of earth
held the seed.

Then one day in spring
my grandmother shouted,
and we all ran
to the garden
and saw
a beautiful pink lotus
unfurling its petals,
so creamy and soft.

"It is the flower
of life and hope,"
my grandmother said.
"No matter how
ugly the mud
or how long the seed
lies dormant,
the bloom will
be beautiful.
It is the flower
of my country."

When the lotus blossom
faded and turned
into a pod,
Bà gave each of
her grandchildren
a seed
to remember her by,
and she kept one
for herself
to remember the emperor by.

I wrapped my seed
in a piece of silk
and hid it
in a secret place.
Someday I will plant it
and give the seeds
to my own children
and tell them about the day
my grandmother saw
the emperor cry.

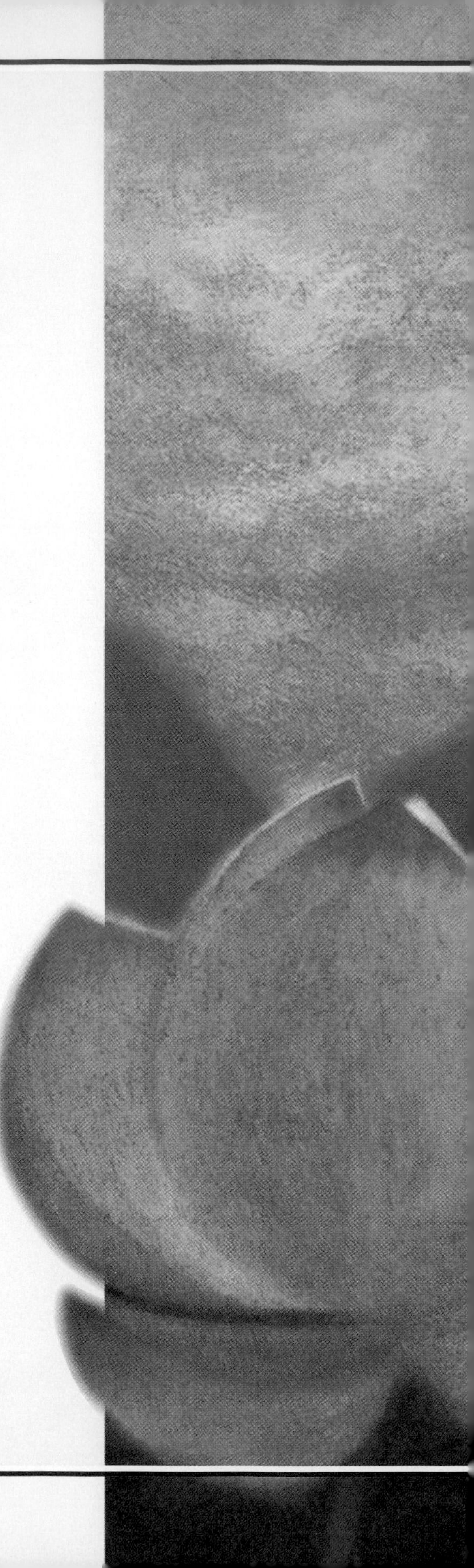

Sherry Garland
Talks About The Lotus Seed

Writer Ilene Cooper interviewed Sherry Garland.

Ilene Cooper: The Lotus Seed *is about people from Vietnam. Have you ever visited that country?*

Sherry Garland: No, although I would like to very much. But I have come to know many Vietnamese people.

Cooper: *Where did the idea for* The Lotus Seed *come from?*

Garland: I had written a novel for adults in which a Vietnamese woman carries a lotus seed. That novel was never published. One day, the idea of the woman and her lotus seed came back to me. In one sitting, I wrote the children's book.

Cooper: *The illustrator of this book, Tatsuro Kiuchi, is Japanese. How did he do his work?*

Garland: I sent him photos of Vietnamese clothing and other things, and he worked from those. The publisher even sent him a lotus flower because he had never seen one.

Cooper: *What do Vietnamese people think of your book?*

Garland: I don't know how the people in Vietnam would feel about it. But Vietnamese Americans I have shown it to like it very much. Older people, especially those who actually came from Vietnam, remember their growing-up years fondly and talk about their country all the time.

Response Corner

SYMBOLS OF AMERICA

A bald eagle, the Statue of Liberty, and the American flag are all symbols that have special meanings to Americans. Research one of these symbols. Write a short report about your choice, and present it to your classmates.

TREASURES

In "The Lotus Seed," the grandmother has to leave her homeland in a hurry. She has to leave many things behind. If *you* had to leave your home quickly, what three things would you take with you? Write a diary entry explaining your choice.

OUR ROOTS

Sometimes young people have a hard time understanding the past. Imagine that the grandmother in the story wants to explain to her grandson what the lotus seed means to the family. Write a letter in which she tells how she felt on the day she thought the seed was lost forever. Then have her tell how she felt when the lotus flower bloomed.

What Do You Think?

- Why does the person telling this story hide her own lotus seed at the end?

- How do you think the grandmother feels when she first moves to this country? Why do you think as you do?

- People come to America from all over the world. What kinds of things do they keep to remind them of their old homes or of how their families used to live?

Art & Literature

I n the 1800s, most immigrants to the United States arrived in New York by ship. Traveling across the ocean took much longer then, and the ships were not as clean and dry as modern ships. How do you think the people in this painting felt when they reached America?

Museum of the City of New York,
Gift of Mrs. Robert M. Littlejohn; 8'1" x 16'6"

The Bay and Harbor of New York
by Samuel B. Waugh

Samuel B. Waugh was born in Mercer, Pennsylvania. He spent many years in Italy, but he did most of his work in Philadelphia. No one knows exactly when *The Bay and Harbor of New York* was painted, but it was probably close to 1855.

Amber Brown
IS NOT A CRAYON

by Paula Danziger
illustrated by Tony Ross

Award-Winning Author

Amber Brown and Justin Daniels have been best friends since preschool. They even sit together on the imaginary trips Mr. Cohen's class takes to different parts of the world. Amber thinks her year is going great until she learns that Justin is moving to Alabama. One day while Justin is packing a box of important items, the two friends get into an argument about keeping a chewing gum ball that they have been adding to for a year and a half. Will they make up?

Today, Mr. Cohen's class is going to have a pizza party.

That's the good news.

The bad news is that it's a going-away party for my ex-best friend, Justin Daniels, and we still haven't spoken to each other.

I've been waiting for him to say "I'm sorry."

I don't know what he's been waiting for.

So we've been sitting in class right next to each other without saying a word.

Well, hardly a word.

I confess. Once I did say, "Hey, dirt bag. Would you please pass the eraser?"

And he said, "Crayon brain, get your own eraser."

It hurts a lot but I'm not going to give in on this one.

Justin is just so stubborn.

Today, the class "returned" from our trip to China.

Next we'll be "going" to Australia.

I can't wait.

Justin, however, won't be "going." He'll be going to Alabama for real.

I wish Al Abama was a real person so I could tell him how much I hate him.

As Brandi Colwin walks by our desks, I call out, "Hey, Brandi. Don't forget. We're going to sit next to each other when we go to Australia."

Then Justin turns to Hannah and says, "I'll be sure to send you some postcards from Alabama."

I yawn, a big yawn, right in his face, to show I don't care, and then I pretend to scrunch up over my worksheet so that he can't see that I'm very close to crying.

Mr. Cohen flicks the lights off and on.

"The pizza will be here in five minutes. Extra cheese, mushrooms, the works."

I pick up my head and look over at Justin. He doesn't look any happier than I feel.

I make a decision and call out, "Tell the guy to hold the anchovies," and then look right at Justin, pretending to be holding wiggly anchovies.

He starts to laugh.

I pretend to flip an anchovy over to him.

He pretends to grab it.

"Let's go stand in the hall for a minute," Justin says, picking up his knapsack.

We both walk over to Mr. Cohen and ask to go out in the hall for a few minutes.

"Sure." He motions to the door.

As we walk out, I think I hear Mr. Cohen say, "Finally."

Once we get out there, we just stand quietly for a few minutes.

Then we both say "I'm sorry" at the same time and link pinkies.

"I don't want you to go." I start to cry, just a little.

Justin takes a deep breath and says, "I don't want to go either. You think this is easy? My new school is so big. I don't know anyone there. What if I forget my locker combination? All the kids there already know each other. My parents say I have to be brave, to be a good example for Danny. That it will be fun. But I know my mom is nervous about moving, too. I heard her talking to your mom. And it's too late to join a little league team, and everyone there thinks I talk funny and I have to learn to say 'Y'all' and 'Ma'am,' and . . . and . . ."

I say, "And?"

Justin turns red. "And I'm going to miss you."

I smile for what seems like the first time in years.

We stand for a few minutes and then I say, "Why didn't you tell me that sooner?"

"Because you stopped talking to me," he says.

"You wouldn't talk to me." I defend myself. "Not about the important stuff."

"It's hard." He looks down at his untied shoelaces.

I say, "I want you to stay."

Justin looks up. "Me, too. But I can't. My parents are making me go. But they said you and your mom could visit this summer."

This summer. I better start practicing "Y'all" and "Ma'am."

Justin pulls something out of his knapsack.

It's a badly wrapped present.

I open the package.

It's a tissue box.

Inside the tissue box is the chewing gum ball.

"Thanks. It's the best present ever," I say, knowing that I will save it for the rest of my life.

The pizza guy arrives with ten pizzas. My stomach smells the extra cheese. Mr. Cohen comes out.

"You two better get inside before everyone eats up all of this pizza. It's your party, Justin."

As we walk inside, I think about how it will be when Justin and I grow up and he doesn't have to move just because his parents move.

Maybe someday we can open our own company. I'll be president one week and he'll be president the next. We'll sell jars of icing and boxes of cookies.

Maybe someday we'll travel around the world trying out new flavors of chewing gum, and the chewing gum ball will get so big that we'll build a house for it.

Until then, maybe, I can save some of my allowance each week and call Justin once in a while. He can do the same.

I think I'm going to learn his new phone number by heart.

Whenever I think about third grade, I'm going to think about Justin, and I bet he's always going to think about me.

SAY HELLO TO
Paula Danziger

Paula Danziger knew in the second grade that she wanted to be a writer. That's when she began noticing and remembering things that happened to her so she could write about them later.

During Paula's childhood, her family moved a lot. She lived in Washington, D.C., in New Jersey, and in a rented farmhouse in Pennsylvania. Paula read books all the time. "Thank goodness for the local librarian. She gave me lots of wonderful books to read, and she let me know she cared."

Paula Danziger was once a teacher, and she uses her teaching experiences in her writing. Some of the events in her books come from real things that happened in her classroom. "What matters to me is that kids like my books, and that my books touch their lives and make them feel less alone."

Map It Out

Amber will have a friend in another part of the country. On a map, find the places where your family and friends live. In what direction would you travel to get to their homes? About how far would you have to travel? Use the distance scale and the compass rose to help you. Share your findings with your family and classmates.

Response Corner

WRITE AN ADVICE COLUMN

Make Up and Be Friends

Friends sometimes have disagreements. With a partner, talk about why friends might disagree and how they can make up. Write an advice column about disagreements. Take turns writing and answering the questions. Share your "column" with your class.

TELL JOKES

Joking Around

A sense of humor can help you make and keep friends. It worked for Amber! Look through some joke books to find jokes that you think others might enjoy. Read a few of them to your class.

What Do You Think?

■ What problem must Amber Brown face?

■ Would you like to read more about Amber Brown? Why or why not?

■ Justin is nervous about moving. How do you think he will feel about his new home a year from now? Why do you think so?

When Jo Louis

by Belinda Rochelle

illustrated by Larry Johnson

Award-Winning
Author

Won the Title

Jo Louis sat perched on the top step of ten steps, waiting for her grandfather, John Henry.

"Is that my favorite girl in the whole wide world?" he said as he strolled up the street. He leaned over and picked up Jo Louis, swung her round and round until her ponytails whirled like the propellers of a plane, swung her round and round until they were both dizzy with gasps, swung her round and round until they were both dizzy with giggles.

John Henry's brown eyes twinkled as he returned Jo Louis to the top step and sat down next to her. The smile quickly disappeared from Jo Louis's face. "Why such a sad face on a pretty girl?" he asked.

Tomorrow was a special day for Jo Louis. The first day at a new school. "I don't want to go to school!" Jo Louis said to her grandfather. "I don't want to be the new girl in a new neighborhood at a new school."

John Henry put his arm around her and pulled her close.

"Why don't you want to go to school?" he asked.

"I'll probably be the shortest kid in class, or I'll be the one who can't run as fast as the other kids. I finish every race last."

"It's just a matter of time before a new school is an old school. Just a matter of time before you'll be able to run really fast, and you won't always finish last," he said, patting her hand. "What's the real reason you don't want to go to school?" John Henry asked.

Jo Louis shook her head. It was hard to explain. She just knew it would happen. Someone would ask THE question. IT was THE question, the same question each and every time she met someone new: *"What's your name?"*

It was that moment, that question, that made Jo Louis want to disappear. And it really wouldn't make a difference if she were taller, and it wouldn't make a difference that she was the new kid in school, and it wouldn't make a difference if she could run really fast. She just wished that she didn't have to tell anyone her name.

Her grandfather picked her up and placed her on his knee. "Let me tell you a story," he said.

"When I was just a young boy living in Mississippi," he began, "I used to dream about moving north. To me it was the promised land. I wanted to find a good job in the big city. Cities like Chicago, St. Louis. But everybody, I mean everybody, talked about Harlem in New York City. Going north, it was all anybody ever talked about. I would sit on the front porch and just daydream about those big-city places. The way some folks told it everything was perfect. Even the streets in the big city were paved with gold, and it was all there just waiting for me." John Henry's eyes sparkled as his voice quickened. "When I saved enough money, I crowded onto the train with other small-town folks headed north. Everything I owned fit into a torn, tattered suitcase and a brown box wrapped in string.

"I rode the train all day and all night. Like a snake winding its way across the Mississippi River, that train moved slowly through farmlands and flatland, over mountains and valleys, until it reached its final destination."

Jo Louis closed her eyes. She loved her grandfather's stories—his words were like wings and other things. She listened closely until she felt she was right there with him.

209

"'New York City! New York! New York!'
the conductor bellowed as the train pulled
into the station.

"I headed straight to Harlem. I had never
seen buildings so tall. They almost seemed
to touch the sky. Even the moon looked
different in the big city. The moonlight
was bright and shining, the stars
skipped across the sky.

"The streets sparkled in the night sky's light. It was true! The streets did seem to be paved in gold! I walked up and down city streets that stretched wide and long. I walked past a fancy nightclub, where you could hear the moaning of a saxophone and a woman singing so sad, so soft, and so slow that the music made me long for home.

"And then, all of a sudden the sad
music changed to happy music.
That saxophone and singing started to swing.
Hundreds of people spilled out into the
sidewalks, waving flags, scarves,
waving handkerchiefs and tablecloths.
Hundreds of people filled the streets
with noise and laughter, waving hats and
anything and everything, filling the sky with
bright colors of red, white, green, yellow,
blue, purple, and orange.

"Everybody was clapping,
hands were raised high to the sky.
Up and down the street,
people were shouting and singing.
Cars were beeping their horns;
bells were ringing.

'Excuse me.' I patted a woman on the shoulder.
'What's going on?' I asked.
The woman smiled.
She was pretty with soft, brown hair
and a friendly smile.
'Why, haven't you heard?' she said,
'Joe Louis won the title fight.
My name is Mary'—she held out
her hand—'and your name is…?' "

John Henry smiled and hugged Jo Louis close.
"It was a special night for me. It was a special
night for black people everywhere.
Joe Louis was the greatest boxer in the world.
He was a hero. That night he won the fight
of his life. A fight that a lot of people thought
he would lose. Some folks said he was too slow,
others said he wasn't strong enough.
But he worked hard and won. It was a special
night, my first night in the big city, and
Joe Louis won the fight. But the night
was special for another reason."

"It was the night you met Grandma,"
Jo Louis said, and she started to smile.

"It was a special night that I'll never forget.
I named your father Joe Louis, and he
named you, his first child, Jo Louis, too."
Her grandfather tickled her nose.
"That was the night you won the title.
You should be very proud of your name.
Every name has a special story."

The next day Jo Louis took a deep breath as she walked into her new school classroom and slipped into a seat.
The boy sitting next to Jo Louis tapped her on the shoulder.
"My name is Lester. What's your name?"

Jo answered slowly, "My name is Jo . . . Jo Louis."
She balled her fist and closed her eyes and braced herself.
She waited, waited for the laughter, waited for the jokes.
She peeked out of one eye, then she peeked out the other eye.

"Wow, what a great name!" he said, and smiled.

Author
Belinda Rochelle

Belinda Rochelle

Belinda Rochelle loves sports.
"I remember my grandmother telling
me stories about Joe Louis," she says,
"and about what his fights meant to
African Americans." Years later, Belinda
Rochelle used her grandmother's stories to
help her write *When Jo Louis Won the Title*.

Belinda Rochelle's first writing project was
about another famous American—Abraham
Lincoln. When she was in sixth grade, she
wrote a play for her class about President
Lincoln. That's when Belinda knew
that she wanted to become a writer.

Illustrator Larry Johnson

When Larry Johnson was in third
grade, he learned two important
things about himself. The first was that he
loved sports. The second was that he had a
talent for art. So he began making drawings
about sports and sports figures.

When Jo Louis Won the Title isn't really a sports
story, but Larry Johnson's love of sports made him
a "natural" to illustrate it. The fact
that he is a grandfather made the
job even more fun for him!

Larry Johnson

217

Being the New Kid

How would you feel if you were Jo Louis, in a new neighborhood and a new school? Work with a group to make a poster for new students like Jo Louis. Write ten tips that could help a new student feel at home in your school.

Response Corner

RETELL A FOLKTALE

Legends of the Past

Jo Louis's grandfather was named for John Henry, an African American folk hero. Read the folktale about John Henry, and find a copy of the song about him. Retell the tale to your classmates. If you like to sing, perform the song as well.

Harlem Heroes

Jo's grandfather was raised in Mississippi, but he traveled to Harlem in New York City. Many other African Americans traveled to Harlem at the same time. Look up Harlem in an encyclopedia. Start a picture gallery of famous African Americans who have lived in this community. Draw their faces, and add information about why they are important.

What Do You Think?

• How does her grandfather's story make Jo Louis feel?

• Jo Louis was worried that she would be teased about her name. Why is it wrong for children to tease each other about their names?

• How did the people in New York City feel about the fighter Joe Louis? Is there a sports star who is important to your community? Why is that person important?

Theme Wrap-Up

Why do you think some people want to travel to new places? Why do some people prefer to stay home? Think about the characters in this theme to help you answer.

If Great-Aunt Arizona met Jo Louis, what do you think they would say to each other? Why do you think so?

ACTIVITY CORNER

Find out about newcomers in your town or city, or in a city nearby. First, call or write to the Chamber of Commerce. Ask how many people have moved to the area in the past five years. Then, find out where most of the newcomers came from. Share your results with your classmates.

Exploring Challenges

We can explore space because creative inventors and scientists have thought of new ways to make rockets, cameras, and other tools. Creative people also think about new ways to solve problems here on Earth. As you read the selections in this theme, think about creative ways to solve problems and meet challenges in your everyday life.

THEME
Exploring Challenges

Contents

Bookshelf

Max Malone Makes a Million
by Charlotte Herman

Max and his friend Gordy are determined to earn a million dollars.

Signatures Library

Julian's Glorious Summer
by Ann Cameron

Julian's friend Gloria gets a new bike. It seems that Julian is downright unhappy when his father also buys him a new bike.

Award-Winning Author

Signatures Library

What's Out There?
A Book About Space
by Lynn Wilson

Explore the Sun, the Moon, and the planets, and learn about how they move.

Cam Jansen and the Mystery of the Television Dog
by David A. Adler

Cam and her friends meet a famous pooch—who then disappears.
Award-Winning Illustrator

Sam and the Lucky Money
by Karen Chinn

Sam has trouble deciding how to spend his special holiday money— until he finds a truly good use for it.

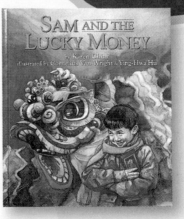

Russell Stannard is Professor of Physics at the Open University in Britain. In his spare time, he builds large sculptures in his backyard.

JOURNEY THROUGH THE

BY RUSSELL STANNARD

SOLAR SYSTEM

Leaving Home

Come with me on a journey to the far depths of space. I shall show you the solar system.

There are so many strange and wonderful things to understand, so many mysteries to unravel—not only about the universe, but also about ourselves and our place in the world.

What do we need for the trip? Imagination. There's no other way to make this journey. No spaceship ever built (or ever likely to be built) can take us where we wish to go. But even though the trip has to be an imaginary one, scientists are fairly sure this is what such a journey would be like . . .

Just a Minute!

Before we blast off into space, let's think for a moment. The Earth we live on is part of the universe we wish to explore. Except for the Moon, and possibly the nearby planets, it is the only part of the universe we can actually get our hands on. The laws of nature that rule everything going on here might be the same laws that apply everywhere else. So why not take a quick look around here on Earth, before we launch out into the unknown?

Round or Flat?

First of all, there is the shape of the Earth. Long ago, everyone thought the Earth was flat—apart from the odd hill or valley, of course. There's no doubt it looks flat. At the seaside the water seems to stretch on forever, as far as the eye can see.

But suppose on a clear day we look through a pair of binoculars at a distant ship. As it travels away from us, it seems to sink as it disappears over the horizon.

This is because the Earth is actually round. It is a ball 7,926 miles (12,756 km) across.

Going Down

Right under our feet, nearly 8,000 miles (13,000 km) down, is the other side of the Earth. What keeps the people who live there from falling off?

First we have to stop thinking that there is some special direction in space called "down," such that everything is pulled in that direction. All directions in space are similar to one another. The important thing is that when something falls, it falls toward the Earth—it is the Earth that does the pulling.

To do this, our planet uses a force, an invisible one, called gravity. The strength of this force depends on how far away you are from the Earth. The bigger the distance, the weaker the force. If you go twice the distance away from the Earth's center, the force drops to a quarter; three times the distance, a ninth; ten times the distance, a hundredth; and so on. But although it gets weaker and weaker, it never completely disappears; it stretches out into space, to infinity.

The force is strongest on the surface of the Earth. Gravity is what holds you down in your seat at this very moment. If you get up and jump, gravity will pull you back again.

Although the Earth is round, it's not a perfect sphere—it bulges slightly at the equator. The diameter through the center of the Earth is 7900 miles from pole to pole, but 7926 miles across the equator.

Now, if you and I are pulled toward the center of the Earth, the same will be true of everyone else, wherever they are on the surface of the Earth. They will all talk about being pulled "down." But all their "downs" are different.

The Force That Shapes the Universe

It is not just the things outside the Earth that feel the pull of gravity; the stuff that makes up the Earth itself feels it too. Every part of the Earth is pulling on every other part of it. That's why the Earth ends up round; it's the best way of packing things together so that

"How come people on the other side of the world don't fall off?"

Gravity makes every part of the Earth pull on every other part and tries to drag them all to the center. That's why our planet is round.

they can all get as close as possible to one another. All the bits of rock and dirt try to get to the center of the Earth, but they are stopped by others that got there first.

Why am I telling you this? The point is, even before we get in our rocket and leave the Earth, we already have some idea of what we are likely to find out on our travels. If the Earth attracts everything with gravity, then perhaps everything we'll come across in space attracts everything else with gravity. In fact, we shall find *it is the force of gravity that shapes the entire universe.* Not only that, but if being round is the most practical shape for the Earth, then most things out there are likely to be round too.

Looking Up

When we look up at the sky, to where we shall soon be heading, what do we see? The Sun, the Moon, and the stars. They are all moving slowly across the sky and around our planet. Or are they? They certainly appear to be. But people have been fooled by appearances before. Learning things often involves unlearning things first. (Remember the "down" that wasn't everyone's "down.")

For example, people used to think the sky was a great hollow dome, with twinkly lights (the stars) stuck to it. They were amazed to learn that it wasn't so. Not only that, but the stars, the Sun, and the Moon were not going around the Earth once every 24 hours. It was the Earth that was spinning. The Earth completes one of its turns every 24-hour day.

When people still believed everything went around the Earth, we thought we were at the center of the universe. That meant we human beings must be very important. We *are* important (at least, I think so), but not for that reason. This is an example of the way discoveries about the universe can raise interesting questions about ourselves.

The fact that the Earth spins like a top leads us to expect that most other things we shall discover in our travels will also be spinning.

Where To?

The largest objects in the sky are, of course, the Sun and Moon. They appear to be roughly the same size. But again we must be careful. The apparent size of something depends on how far away it is.

> The Moon is almost 400 times closer to the Earth than the Sun is, and 100 times closer than the nearest planet.

In fact, the Moon is much closer. It is our nearest neighbor in space. So it sounds like a good place, at long last, to start our space journey.

FIRST STOP
THE MOON

Three... two... one... blast off!

As we approach the Moon, the first thing we notice is that it is a round ball; it is not a flat disk, which is what it looks like from Earth. (But a round ball is the shape we expect from gravity, right?)

Secondly, the Man in the Moon has disappeared! His face, with those staring eyes and the open mouth which always seems to be saying "Oooh," has broken up into mountains and valleys pitted with deep holes and craters. These were made by meteoroids, thousands of rocks that fly through space and crash into anything that gets in their way.

Unlike the meteoroids, we land our craft gently.

The Moon's diameter is 2,160 mi. (3,476 km). That is roughly equal to the distance across Australia. It would take 81 Moons to weigh the same as Earth.

Twelve astronauts walked on the Moon between 1969 and 1972. Their footprints are still there, in the moon-dust that covers the surface. This is because there is no wind and rain to wear them away

Going for a Stroll

Walking on the Moon is fun. You feel very light. You can take big, big steps. And boy how you can jump! Six times as high as on the Earth.

This is because the Moon's gravity force is not as strong as the Earth's—only one-sixth. Your weight depends on the gravity force. If gravity is only one-sixth as strong, your weight on the Moon will be only one-sixth of your weight on the Earth.

Why is the Moon's gravity so much less than the Earth's? The Moon does not have as much mass as the Earth; it is not as heavy. In the first place, it is smaller. In the second, the material from which it is made has a lower density; it is not packed together as tightly as the Earth's material.

But although the Moon's gravity is weak, notice that *it does have a gravity force.* (Don't be fooled by those pictures of astronauts floating around weightless inside their spacecraft.) Remember, *everything* has a gravity force.

Give Me Air!

Because the Moon's gravity is so weak, there is no atmosphere here; the Moon can't hold on to one. The atmosphere, if there ever was one, just floated away. There is no air, no water, no life—all very different from the Earth.

This is why astronauts must wear space suits on the Moon; they have to carry their own supply of air to breathe.

The Far Side

Just as the Earth spins around like a top as it orbits the Sun, so the Moon spins too. It takes 27.3 days, roughly one month, to spin around once, which is the same time it takes to orbit the Earth. And that means we always see the same side of the Moon on Earth. We call this side the near side. Until a spacecraft sent back photographs in 1959, no one had ever seen the far side. What did the photos show? Oddly, many many more craters than on the near side.

And now we must leave the Moon. "Already?" you ask. I'm afraid so. Quite frankly, our travels have much more exciting things in store!

THE SUN: A BOMB THAT GOES OFF SLOWLY

As seen from the Earth, the Moon and the Sun may look similar. In fact, they are very different. The Moon is a round dusty rock; the Sun is a huge ball of flaming hot gas. And I do mean huge; the distance from one side of the Sun to the other, its diameter, is 865,000 miles (1.4 million km). That is 109 times the diameter of the Earth. The reason it doesn't look a lot bigger than the Moon is that the Sun is much farther away.

Because the Sun's gas is so hot, it swirls and rushes and jiggles around a lot. You might think that all this movement

More than one million Earths could fit inside the Sun.

would throw the gas off into space. But no. The Sun has 333,000 times the mass of the Earth, and it has an *enormous* gravity force. It is this force that keeps the gas together.

Next Stop, the Sun?

take-off. . .

Just as the Moon orbits the Earth, so the Earth orbits the Sun. It does this once every 365 days—in other words, once a year. And it stays at a distance of roughly 93 million miles (150 million km) from the Sun. That is a long way. A spacecraft traveling at the speed of a jumbo jet would take about 20 years to get to the Sun. (That's a lot of inflight movies!) If, like an airplane flight, the fare was based on a rate of about 18 cents per mile, a one-way ticket would cost nearly $17 million!

As you approach the Sun (but not too closely!), you'll see that its surface is anything but smooth and regular. The flaming hot gas is always seething and swirling about. Some of the gas leaps up high; these are called solar prominences. The surface is also marked by darker patches known as sunspots; these are regions of somewhat cooler gas.

. . . arrival

Spring, Summer, Fall, Winter

The Earth's orbit around the Sun is almost a circle, but not quite. It is slightly squashed. We call its oval shape an ellipse. So our distance from the Sun varies slightly during the year it takes us to complete the orbit. Is this why we have hot weather in summer and cold in winter?

No. The effect of this varying distance is very tiny. The real reason for the different seasons has to do with the way the Earth spins while it is orbiting the Sun. As we have already learned, the Earth spins like a top. It does this around an imaginary line that joins the North and South poles and is called the axis.

Looking at the diagram, you can see how this North-South axis is tilted to one side. Suppose it was *not* like this. Suppose it was bolt upright. Then there would be no seasons; the weather would stay the same all year round. The only effect of spinning would be to give us night and day—night when we were facing away from the Sun, day when we faced toward it.

But that is not how the axis is arranged. It is tilted. So, if we live in the North, at one stage of the orbit the axis tends to tip us slightly toward the Sun—the Sun beats down on us and we get long, hot summer days. Meanwhile, those living in the South are pointed away from the Sun; its rays hit them at only a glancing angle, and that's when they get their winter. On the opposite side of the orbit, six months later, we change places; it is then our turn to have winter, and theirs to have summer.

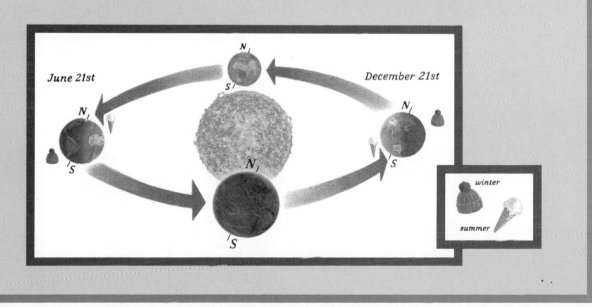

Phew! It's Hot!

It's a good thing we stay a long way from the Sun. The temperature of its surface is about 10,000°F (5,500°C).

And that is just the temperature of the surface. Deep down inside the Sun, the temperature increases. It becomes hotter and hotter, until right at the very center of the Sun the temperature is 27 million°F (15 million°C).

The temperature of ice is 32°F (0°C) and boiling water is 212°F (100°C). Think about how hot 10,000°F (5,500°C) must be!

The Sun's Central Heating System

● ● ● ● ● ● ● ● ● ● ● ● ● ● ● ● ● ● ●

The Sun pours out heat and light all the time. How does it manage to do this and still stay hot? What kind of fuel does it use to keep its fires burning? The answer is nuclear fuel—which stores the same kind of energy you get in a hydrogen bomb.

The heart of the fire is deep down in the central core of the Sun. It has been burning for 4.6 billion years. When you stop to think about it, that is really quite amazing. A hydrogen bomb going off *slowly*!

There are times when it appears as if the Sun's great fire has gone out. This is when the Moon passes between us and the Sun and blocks our view of the Sun. We call this an eclipse. When will the Sun's fire *really* go out? The Sun has enough fuel to last another 5 billion years.

Sunlight takes 8.3 minutes to reach Earth. That means the Sun you see now is actually how the Sun looked 8.3 minutes ago. (But you should never look directly at the Sun—it could blind you!)

VISITING THE NEIGHBORS

The Earth is not the only planet going around the Sun. There are eight others. And what a mixed bunch they are!

NEPTUNE

EARTH

VENUS

SUN

MERCURY

MARS

JUPITER

The Planets Next Door

We start with Mercury, the planet closest to the Sun. It races around the Sun at 30 miles (48 km) per second, completing its orbit in only 88 days instead of the Earth's sluggardly 365. Like all the planets, Mercury is also spinning on its axis. It spins more slowly than the Earth, taking 59 days for a full turn instead of one. This makes it look as if the Sun is passing across the sky incredibly slowly. So much so that Mercury's "day" (from noon one day to noon the next) is twice as long as its "year" (one orbit around the Sun). That means you would get two birthdays every day!

SATURN

245

Mercury

Diameter: 3,032 mi.
Average distance from Sun:
36 million mi.
Speed:
30 mi./second.

But before you rush to set up house on Mercury, think about this: because Mercury is so much closer to the Sun than the Earth is, the Sun looks almost three times as big from this planet. During the day, the temperature is 662°F (350°C); at night it drops to minus 365°F (−221°C). Mercury looks a bit like the Moon, with lots of craters, and like the Moon, it has no atmosphere. It is definitely not the sort of place where I would want to live.

The next planet out from the Sun is Venus. It spins very slowly, in the opposite direction to the Earth's spin.

Venus is about the same size as the Earth and does have an atmosphere. But it is not the type of atmosphere we humans need for breathing. It is mostly a gas called carbon dioxide. One of the interesting things about this gas is the way it prevents heat escaping from the planet; it acts like a thick blanket. The result? The Sun's rays get trapped, and the surface of Venus becomes extremely hot:

860°F (460°C). That is hot enough to melt lead. No other planet is that hot, not even Mercury, the closest to the Sun. But it gets worse. High above this blanket of gas, clouds full of acid rain swirl around the planet, blown along by winds of up to 224 miles (360 km) per hour.

Venus

Diameter: 7,521 mi.
Average distance from Sun:
67 million mi.
Speed:
22 mi./second.

As we continue our journey out from the Sun, we come next to the Earth. I don't have to tell you about that one!

Earth

Diameter: 7,926 mi.
Average distance from Sun:
93 million mi.
Speed: 18.6 mi./second.

Just beyond the Earth's orbit we get to Mars. People used to think that Mars might be a good place to search for life. But space probes have found none. It just seems to be a world of dead volcanoes, craters, very little atmosphere, and raging dust storms. Mars may look red-hot; in fact it's very cold, with an average temperature of minus 58°F (−50°C).

Mars has a couple of very small moons called Phobos and Deimos. These two are so small that they've never had enough gravity to pull all their matter into a tight round ball— that's why they've ended up lumpy and misshapen, like potatoes.

So much for the four rocky planets close to the Sun. Farther out we get four very different planets, all of them HUGE.

Mars

Diameter:
4,217 mi.
Average distance from Sun:
142 million mi.
Speed: 15 mi./second.

A Giant Among Giants

The first is Jupiter—the largest planet of all, with a diameter 11 times that of the Earth. Like the other giant planets, it is mostly a ball of hydrogen and helium. This is in the form of gas at the surface, but deeper down the gas gets packed

Diameter: 88,734 mi.
Average distance from Sun: 484 million mi.
Speed: 8 mi./second.

together so thickly it becomes more like a liquid than a gas. At the center is a core of hot, molten rock, somewhat like the molten lava that comes out of volcanoes on Earth. In other words, there is probably nothing solid about Jupiter, or the other big planets. There's no ground where you can stand and say, "I'm standing on the planet, and what is above me is the planet's atmosphere." In a sense, it is all atmosphere, much like the Sun itself.

When it comes to moons, Jupiter has plenty—16! Ganymede is more than 3,100 miles (5,000 km) across; it's the biggest moon of all.

Icy Rings, Frozen Moons

Next comes Saturn, second in size only to Jupiter. It is famous for being surrounded by many beautiful, wide, flat rings. These are not solid as you might think; they are made up of a vast number of pieces of ice. Some are the size of snowflakes, others are as big as snowballs, and the largest are several yards across. They all move around Saturn in orbit like tiny, tiny moons.

Saturn is not alone in having rings—the other three giant planets also have them. But compared to those of Saturn, they are fewer and much harder to see.

Saturn

Diameter: 74,600 mi.
Average distance from Sun: 870 million mi.
Speed: 6 mi./second.

Saturn also holds the record for moons—18 of them at the last count—though some are very small. One of them, Titan, is large, larger even than planet Mercury. And it has an atmosphere twice as dense as that of Earth. So scientists wonder whether there might be some form of life on this moon. It would be a very simple form because Titan is a long way from the Sun and is very, very cold. It is like an Earth that has been kept in cold storage. We'll have to wait for some future space probe to pay it a visit before we find out whether there's any early form of life there.

Two Blue Giants

As we go deeper still into space, away from the Sun, Uranus is next. Unlike the Earth, which spins on a slightly tilted axis, Uranus spins on its side. It has several narrow rings and 15 moons. Uranus has an atmosphere that is mainly hydrogen, with some helium and methane. Its clouds of methane are what make this planet a lovely shade of blue. Below the

Uranus

Diameter: 32,000 mi.
Average distance from Sun: 1.8 billion mi.
Speed: 4.2 mi./second.

Neptune

Diameter:
30,200 mi.
Average distance from Sun: 2.8 billion mi.
Speed: 3.4 mi./second.

atmosphere there is a rocky core, but whether this is molten or solid is not yet known.

Then comes Neptune, the second blue planet. Savage winds tear across this planet at 1,400 miles (2,200 km) per hour. Far above the storms, eight moons and a few rings orbit more peacefully. One of the moons, Triton, is almost as big as our own Moon. Triton is the coldest place we know—it's minus 390°F (−235°C) there.

P.S. Pluto

Lastly, beyond the giant planets there is Pluto, the smallest planet of all. A ball of rock and ice covered with nitrogen, Pluto has only one-fifth the diameter of Earth. It is so far away that it takes 248 years to complete one huge orbit around the Sun. Pluto has an elliptical orbit, long and squashed and tilted at a different angle from those of the other planets. For 20 years of its orbit Pluto actually comes closer to the Sun than Neptune; for those 20 years Neptune is the most distant planet of all. Another thing about Pluto is that, like Uranus, it spins on its side.

Pluto

Diameter: 1,470 mi.
Average distance from Sun: 3.7 billion mi.
Speed: 2.9 mi./second.

MERCURY It's magic!

Venus

Pluto's moon, Charon, is large for a moon; it is half the diameter of its "parent" planet. Not only that, but it is 20 times closer to Pluto than our Moon is to Earth. Which means that Charon must look huge in the sky over Pluto— seven times bigger than our Moon does over Earth.

The Sun's Family

So there we have it, the nine planets. As I said, a very mixed bunch, varying greatly in size and the stuff from which they are made. They vary in temperature, too—from the 860°F (460°C) heat of Venus to the minus 455°F (−271°C) chill on the surface of distant Neptune.

Note that only one planet has the right kind of temperature and materials to be a home for advanced forms of life: the Earth!

Mars

Wish you were here!

Moonwalk '69

EARTH

I AM FLYING!

BY JACK PRELUTSKY

ILLUSTRATED BY TOM LEONARD

I am flying! I am flying!
I am riding on the breeze,
I am soaring over meadows,
I am sailing over seas,
I ascend above the cities
where the people, small as ants,
cannot sense the keen precision
of my aerobatic dance.

I am flying! I am flying!
I am climbing unconfined,
I am swifter than the falcon,
and I leave the wind behind,
I am swooping, I am swirling
in a jubilant display,
I am brilliant as a comet
blazing through the Milky Way.

I am flying! I am flying!
I am higher than the moon,
still, I think I'd best be landing,
and it cannot be too soon,
for some nasty information
has lit up my little brain—
I am flying! I am flying!
but I fly without a plane.

THE INVENTOR THINKS UP HELICOPTERS

by Patricia Hubbell
illustrated by Ju-Hong Chen

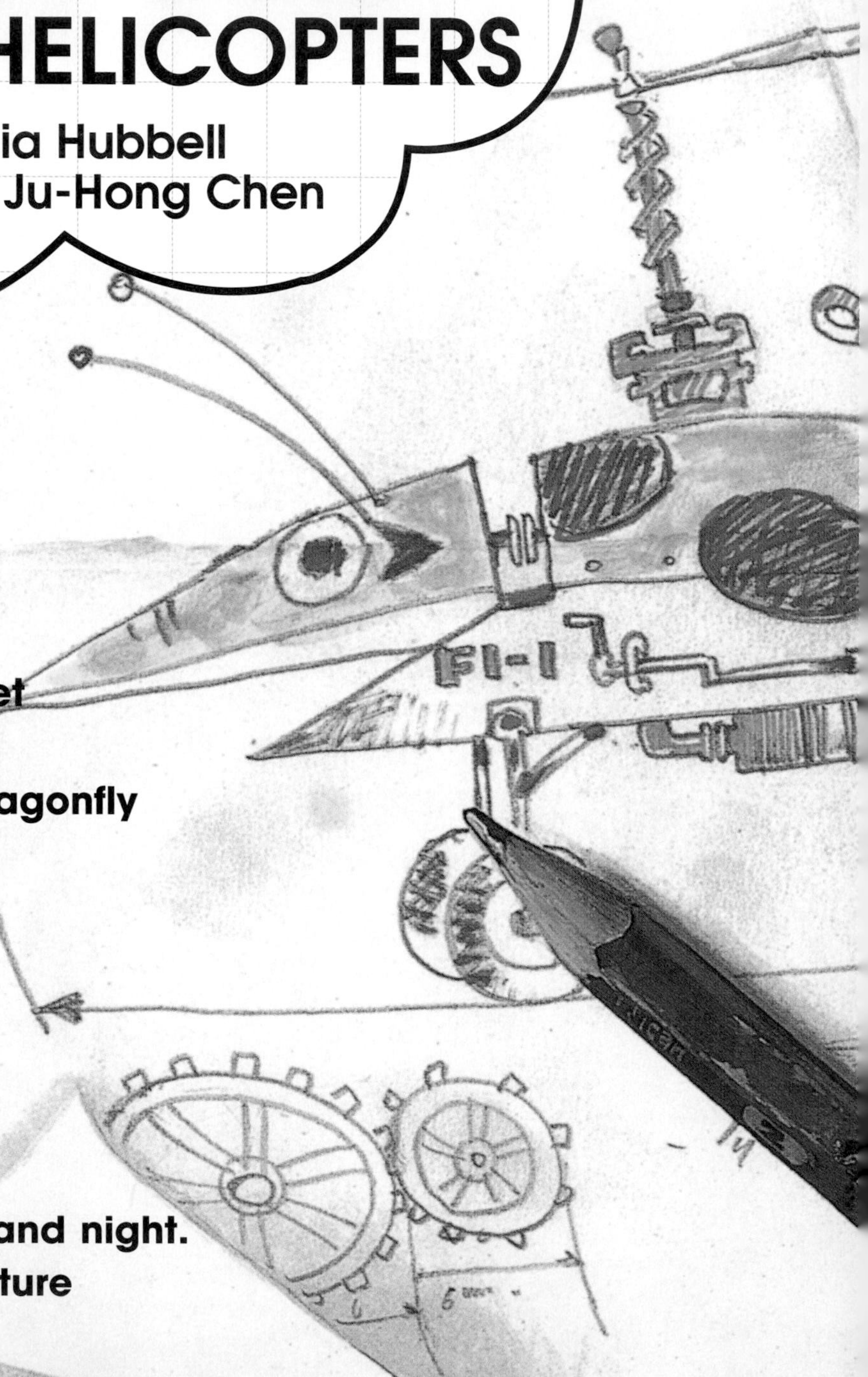

"Why not
a
vertical
whirling
winding
bug,
that hops like a cricket
crossing a rug,
that swerves like a dragonfly
testing his steering,
twisting and veering?
Fleet as a beetle.
Up
down
left
right,
jounce, bounce, day and night.
It could land in a pasture
    the size of a dot . . .
Why not?"

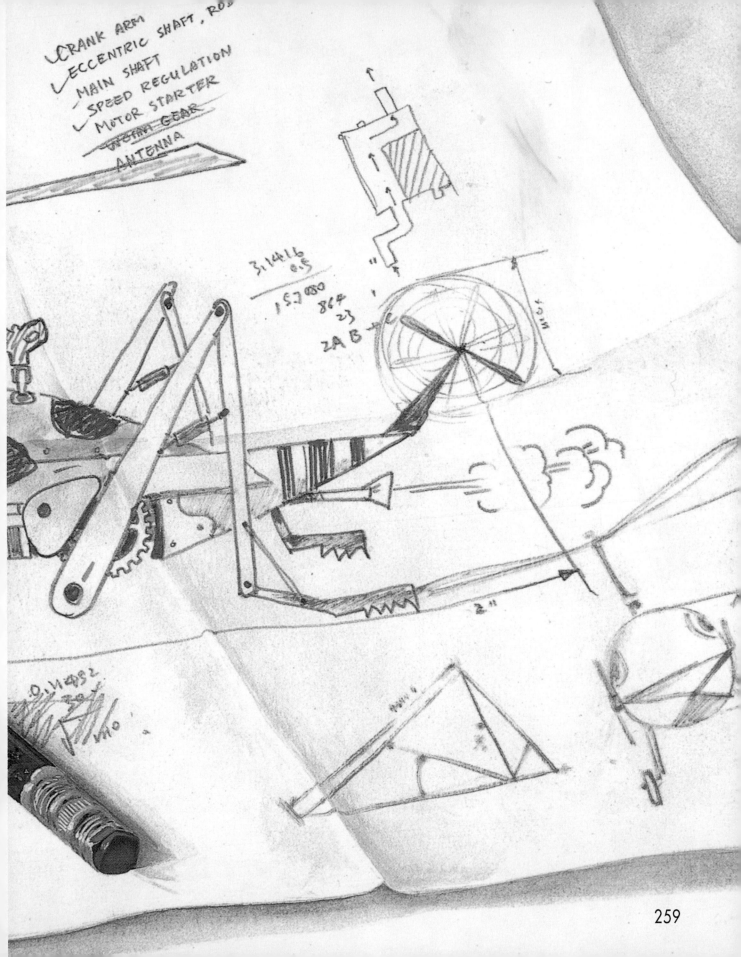

259

RESPONSE

Do You Have the Time?

When it's morning in San Francisco, it's afternoon in New York and evening in London. Find out how many time zones there are in the world. Make a chart that shows the time in each time zone when it is noon where you live. Display your chart in your classroom.

COMPARE AND CONTRAST

Look! Up in the Sky...

Earth is the only planet known to have life. But the other planets, too, have things that are special about them. With a partner, research any two of the other planets and compare them. Find out how they are the same and how they are different. Report your findings to the class.

CORNER

WRITE A SONG

Fly Me to the Moon

There have been many songs written about the Moon. With a partner, make up your own Moon song. Include one fact about the Moon. You might want to make your words fit a tune you know. Sing your song for your classmates.

What Do You Think?

- What do you think the Earth would be like if it were a lot farther away from the Sun?

- What are the most interesting facts you learned in "Journey Through the Solar System"?

- Earth seems to be the only planet in the solar system that has life. Why do you think this is so?

Patently

Which patents did we invent?

Are these inventions for real? Well, eight of them received patents! (The U.S. Patent Office gives patents to inventions that it decides are new and useful. Then, only the inventor can produce that invention.) But a couple of the devices on these pages are fake—we made them up! Can you tell which inventions are real, and which two are phony?

The answers are on page 265.

1. Hats, Caps and Other Head Wear

Patent No. 273,074 (1883)
Want a beautiful headpiece that'll shine in the dark? Dip a hat or cap in special glow-in-the-dark powder. Now your hat will stand out at night. As a bonus, your cap will be easy to spot in dark closets.

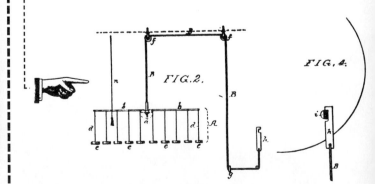

Ridiculous

by Saul T. Prince from *3-2-1 Contact* magazine

2. Device for Waking Persons from Sleep

Patent No. 256,265 (1882)
This is a dream of an alarm clock. Say you set the alarm for 8:00 A.M. At that time, the device lowers towards you. Soon, the corks dangling from its frame bump into your face, gently waking you up.

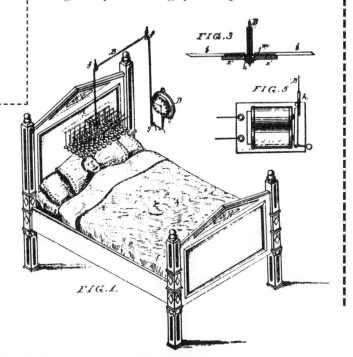

3. Device for Producing Dimples

Patent No. 560,351 (1896)
Dimples are popular. But if you don't have them, you can make them, said the designer of this machine. Just place the knob on your chin or cheek and push the roller around it to form a dimple.

4. Motor Vehicle Attachment

Patent No. 777,369 (1904)

At the turn of the century, cars scared horses on the road. How to keep horses from being spooked was a serious problem. Here's one solution: Attach a fake horse to the front of a car! Then you've turned a scary horseless carriage into a friendly horse-drawn carriage!

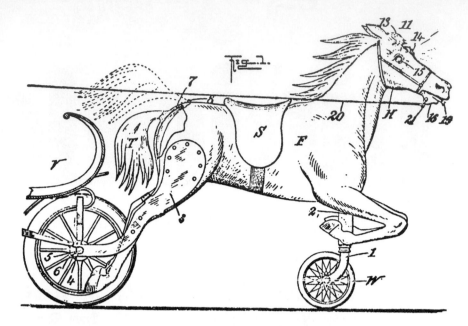

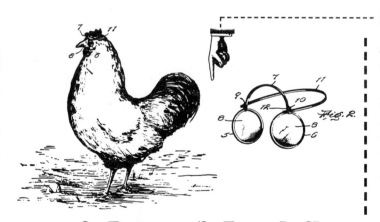

5. Eye Protector for Chickens

Patent No. 730,918 (1903)

These glasses aren't for nearsighted chickens. They're protectors for fighting fowls. They were designed to keep chickens from pecking each other's eyes.

6. Pneumatic Parade Shoes

Patent No. 1,785,406 (1935)

Pressing a button on the shoe fills the heel and sole with air. They stretch out, adding five inches to the wearer's height. This device allows the wearer to see over people's heads at parades and other events.

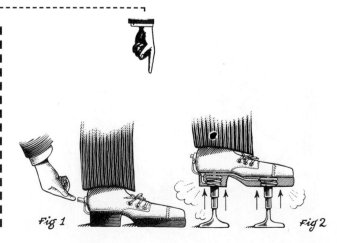

Fig 1   Fig 2

7. Velocipede

Patent No. 190,644 (1870)

This carriage doesn't have horse power—it's got dog power. It operates like a gerbil wheel. Put two dogs inside the vehicle's front wheel. When they run, so does the car.

8. Mouth Opening Alarm

Patent No. 2,999,232 (1961)

This device makes sure you sleep with your mouth closed. When the sleeper's jaw drops, a battery-powered alarm goes off, and the device vibrates. This wakes up the sleeper. After this happens over and over, the person learns to sleep with his or her mouth closed.

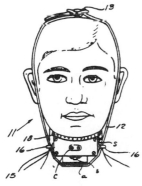

9. Gum Blowing Mouthpiece

Patent No. 2,438,946 (1975)

To blow perfect bubbles, chew some bubble gum and then remove it. Place the plastic device in your mouth. Stretch the bubble gum over the plastic mouthpiece and blow. It can also be worn as a sports mouthpiece—allowing you to blow bubbles while playing basketball, football and other contact sports.

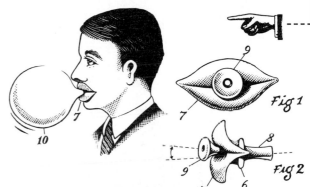

Fig 1

Fig 2

10. Smoker Stopper

Patent No. 3,655,325 (1972)

Want to stop someone from smoking? This machine was designed to snuff out the habit: When you pick up the cigarette package, it starts coughing.

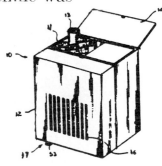

Answers:
The fake inventions are the Pneumatic Parade Shoes (#6) and the Gum Blowing Mouthpiece (#9). Those two devices were illustrated by John Lawrence.

265

Creative Minds

AT WORK

BY JEAN MARZOLLO

Whether we are exploring space or just making life simpler, new inventions can help solve problems. Meet two men who changed the way we live today.

Thomas Alva Edison

(1847–1931)

He invented the electric light bulb, the record player, and many more amazing things.

Thomas Alva Edison was born in Milan, Ohio. The youngest of seven children, he was called Alva. Alva was a curious child, always asking his mother why things worked the way they did. He liked to experiment, too. Once he sat on some goose eggs to see if he could hatch them.

When Alva was seven, his family moved to Michigan. At school, he was whipped by the teacher for asking too many questions. When his mother found this out, she took Alva out of school. From then on, she taught him at home. She had been a teacher and tried to make learning fun for Alva.

As Thomas Alva Edison grew up, he began to invent things. At the age of 23, he figured out a better way to make a telegraph machine. He sold his plan for $40,000. With the money, he opened a workshop, or laboratory, in West Orange, New Jersey. There, he invented a better typewriter. He then moved to Menlo Park,

"WIZARD OF MENLO PARK"

Thomas Alva Edison in his laboratory.

New Jersey, and invented an improved telephone. Thomas Edison invented the record player (called a phonograph) in 1877. Two years later, he invented the electric light bulb. People called him the "Wizard of Menlo Park."

Edison's ears had been injured when he was a young man. As a result, his hearing was poor. As he grew older, his hearing grew worse, but Edison said his deafness helped him concentrate. He was happiest when he was inventing things in his laboratory.

Scientists work in different ways. George Washington Carver mostly worked alone. Marie and Pierre Curie worked together. Thomas Edison liked to work with a team of people. He said that genius was "1 percent inspiration and 99 percent perspiration." With a team of people, the perspiration part of the work could be shared and thus go faster. Edison received many awards for his work.

George Washington Carver

(c. 1864–1943)

He discovered hundreds of new uses for plants.

George Washington Carver was born a slave in Diamond, Missouri. A slave is a person who is owned by someone else. The owner can make the slave work for no pay. In the early history of the United States, white people brought black people from Africa and forced them to work on their farms. When these slaves had children, their birth dates were not always written down. That is why there is a *c* before the date above. It stands for *circa* (SER-ka), which means "about." George Washington Carver was born about 1864.

Shortly after he was born, his father was killed in an accident and his mother was kidnapped. George was raised by his owners. In 1865, when George was one year old and Abraham Lincoln was president, slavery was abolished, or ended. The people who had owned George continued to raise him. They taught him to read and write.

As a child, George loved plants. When he grew up, he went to college and studied agriculture, the science of farming. It was very hard for African Americans to go to college then because many colleges did not accept black people. George Washington Carver worked at different jobs to pay for his education. When he was 32, he was asked to teach at the Tuskegee Institute, a college for African Americans. He taught agricultural students how to grow more plants on their land.

Although he liked teaching, George Washington Carver liked scientific research more. He liked to look at plants and ask, "What would happen if . . . ?" George Washington Carver experimented with peanuts, sweet potatoes, and soybeans in his laboratory. He

George Washington Carver works with students in his laboratory at Tuskegee Institute.

discovered more than 300 different products, including ink, soap, and a milk substitute that could be made from peanuts alone.

George Washington Carver was given many prizes for his research. Toward the end of his life, Carver gave much of the money he had earned to the Tuskegee Institute, so that other scientists could work and study there, too.

Art and Literature

Sometimes we say that people who have big dreams are "reaching for the stars." The scientists and inventors you have read about in this theme had big dreams. What do you think they might have said to the women in this painting? Why?

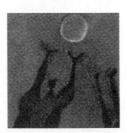

Women Reaching for the Moon (1946)
by Rufino Tamayo

Rufino Tamayo was born in Oaxaca, Mexico, in 1911. He created his own style of painting by combining traditional Mexican art with bold shapes and bright colors.

271

A Class

from KID CITY Magazine
photos by Les Morsillo

YAY!

The kids at Microsociety think their school is the greatest!

272

Act

Microsociety Bank

It's 2 PM at the Microsociety School in Yonkers, New York. It's a very important time of the day. Why? That's when the bank opens! Kids quickly finish their lunch and rush to their jobs as bank tellers. Other kids are getting in line to put their "savings" into their bank accounts. Still others are taking money out of the bank to go shopping, or pay their fines at the Treasury Department.

273

What's Going On?

Kids at the Microsociety School get taught in a very special way. Half the school day is probably very much like yours—with regular classes like math or reading or gym. But the other half is spent the way many grownups spend their days—working and trying to save money.

Can You Lend Me Five Batistas Until Friday?

The kids use fake money instead of real cash. Their money is named after the Superintendent of Schools. For example, it was called "Batistas" when Donald Batista was Superintendent.

Some kids work in the bank, some work in the courtroom, some work in the market on "Market Days." Recycled materials, such as tin cans and paper are used to make stuff that the kids sell to each other. *Kid City* watched as one sales kid said to a customer, "I have a nice change purse here, only ten Batistas!"

Safely in the bank:
Here kids are putting their money in the bank. That's called a deposit. When they take money out, it's called a withdrawal.

What's on sale?

At the Department of Economic Development, kids buy raw materials to make products. Then they sell their stuff to other kids on market day. They sell things like wallets, pencil holders, even jewelry.

Pay Up!

Sometimes there are long lines at the "Department of the Treasury." That's where kids go to pay fines for bad behavior. The kids made up the rules and fines themselves. If you're late for class, you have to pay twenty Batistas. If you run in the hallways, that's fifty Batistas. And don't fight or make noise in the library—that'll cost you *one hundred* Batistas!

School Is Fun!

The school principal, Fred Hernandez, thinks the Microsociety School is a lot of fun for kids. "Teachers usually tell kids to sit down. Be quiet. Don't play," said Mr. Hernandez. "Our school is different because kids get to play every day!" All the kids love their special school, too. "I love going to the bank and going to court," said one kid. "It makes me feel like a grownup!"

Eugenio María de Hostos Micro Society School
Yonkers, NY
100

Eugenio María de Hostos Micro Society School
Yonkers, NY
50

icro Society School
20

Treasury Department

Don't break the law!
Kids go to the Department of the Treasury to pay their fines. They also must pay a monthly tax of forty Batistas.

May I help you?
The kids who work in the bank are happy to help their friends open accounts and fill out their bank books.

CONGRATULATIONS! YOU'VE EARNED A PENNY.

ONE PENNY

It will buy anything that costs one cent.

WELL DONE! YOU'VE MADE A NICKEL.

ONE NICKEL

is worth the same as

FIVE PENNIES

HOORAY! NOW YOU HAVE A DIME.

ONE DIME

has the same value as TWO NICKELS

or TEN PENNIES

EXCELLENT! FOR YOUR HARD WORK YOU'VE EARNED A QUARTER.

ONE QUARTER

is the same amount of money as FIVE NICKELS

or TWO DIMES AND ONE NICKEL

or THREE NICKELS AND ONE DIME

or TWENTY-FIVE PENNIES

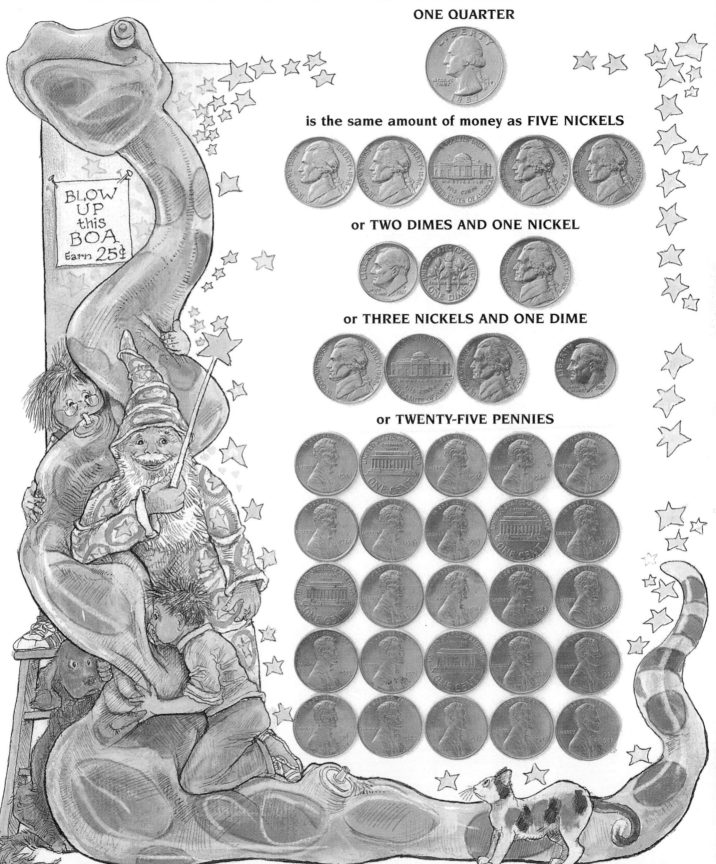

BLOW UP this BOA Earn 25¢

WONDERFUL! YOU ARE NOW A DOLLAR RICHER.

ONE DOLLAR

is worth as much
as FOUR QUARTERS

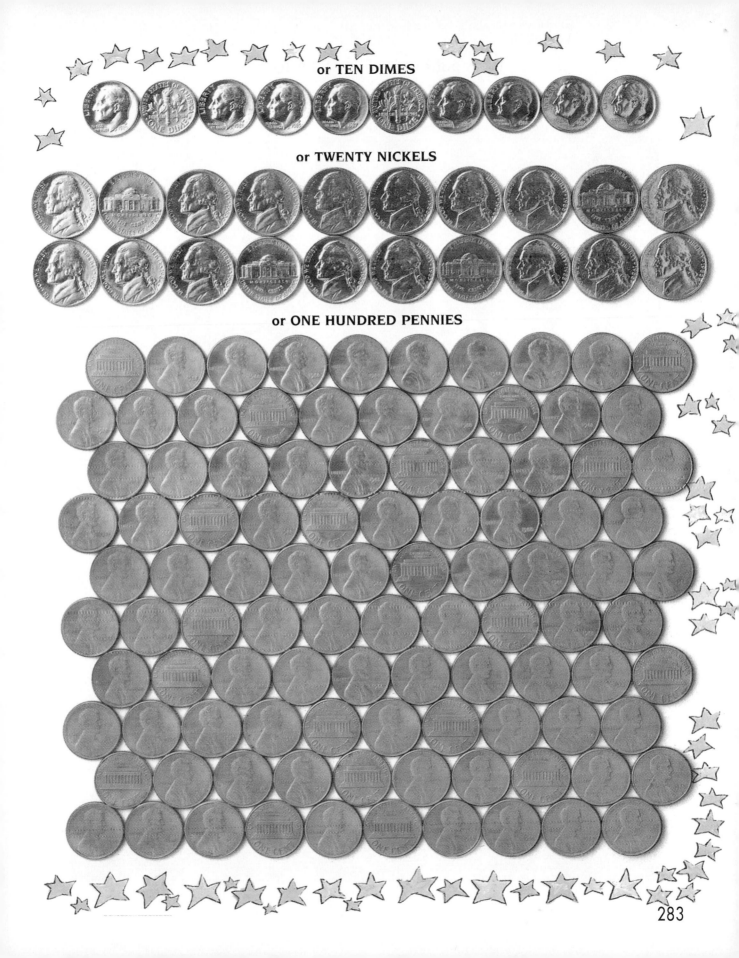

or TEN DIMES

or TWENTY NICKELS

or ONE HUNDRED PENNIES

283

You could use your dollar to buy
one hundred pieces of penny candy,

or twenty five-cent balloons,

or ten stickers for ten cents each,
or four rubber balls that cost
twenty-five cents apiece.

Or perhaps you'd like to save your dollar.
You could put it in the bank,
and a year from now it will be worth $1.05.

The bank wants to use your money,
and it will pay you five cents
to leave your dollar there for a year.
The extra five cents is called interest.

If you waited ten years, your dollar would earn
sixty-four cents in interest just from sitting in the bank.

Are you interested in earning lots of interest? Wait
twenty years, and one dollar will grow to $2.70.

DELICIOUS! YOU'VE BAKED A CAKE AND EARNED FIVE DOLLARS.

You could be paid with one five-dollar bill

or five one-dollar bills. It doesn't matter.
They have the same value.

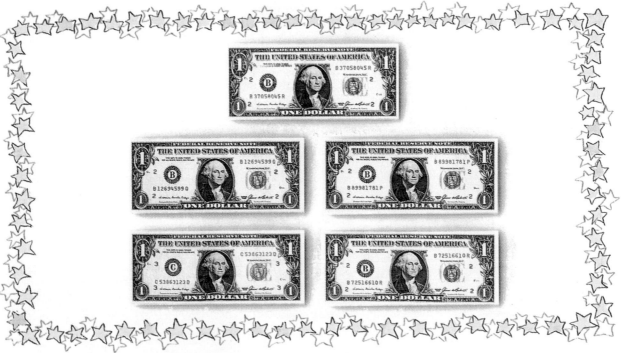

STUPENDOUS! YOU'VE MADE TEN DOLLARS.

How would you like to be paid?

One ten-dollar bill? Two five-dollar bills?

Ten one-dollar bills?

Or perhaps one five and five ones?

Take your pick—they're all worth ten dollars.

If you prefer coins, you can have
a five-foot stack of pennies
(that's one thousand of them) or
a fifteen-inch stack of two hundred nickels.
You could also be paid with one hundred dimes,
which would stack up to just over five inches.
Or you can receive your ten dollars
as a $3\frac{1}{4}$-inch pile of forty quarters.

You could spend your ten dollars on ten kittens or one thousand kitty snacks.

Or you could take your mom to the movies.

But maybe you'd rather save your money.
If you leave your ten dollars in the bank
for ten years, it will earn $6.40 in interest,
and you will have $16.40.

If you leave it there for fifty years,
your ten dollars will grow to $138.02.

YOU'VE WORKED HARD TO EARN
ONE HUNDRED DOLLARS.
You've decided to spend it on a plane ticket
to the beach. You could pay with
a hundred-dollar bill, or two fifty-dollar bills,
or five twenty-dollar bills, or many other
combinations—
six fives, three tens, and two twenties, for instance.

or

or

Paying with pennies?
You'll need ten thousand of them,
and they'll make a fifty-foot stack.

YOU'VE WORKED LONG AND HARD,
AND YOU'VE EARNED A THOUSAND DOLLARS!
You're going to buy a pet.

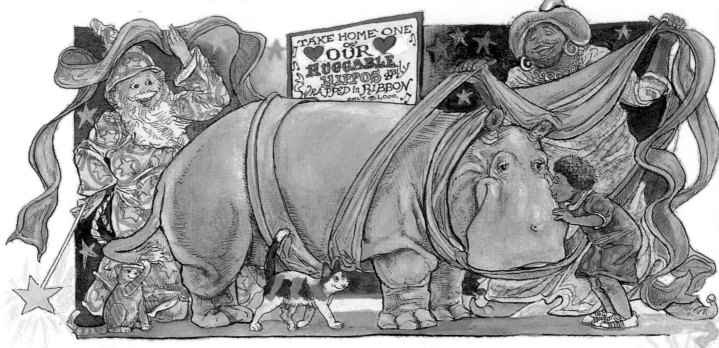

You could pay with coins or bills.

If you don't like the idea of carrying
a thousand dollars around with you,
you can put it in the bank
and pay for the hippo with a check.

The check tells your bank to give $1,000
to the person who sold you the hippo.

Here's how it works: You give the check
to the person who sold you the hippo,
and he gives it to his bank,
and his bank sends it to a very busy
clearinghouse in the city,
and the clearinghouse tells your bank
to take $1,000 out of your money.

After your bank does that,
the clearinghouse tells the hippo salesman's bank
to add $1,000 to his money, so he can take it
and use it whenever, and however, he likes.
Maybe he'll use it to raise more hippos.

If you used pennies to purchase
a $10,000 Ferris wheel,
someone might not be too happy about it.
Even if you used ten thousand one-dollar bills,
they would be mighty hard to handle.

Probably a check would be best.

MAGNIFICENT! YOU'VE EARNED $50,000.
And you've just read about
a well-worn, unloved, but perfectly fixable
castle for sale. The price: $100,000.

The castle costs $100,000 and you have only $50,000.
You're $50,000 short, but you can still buy the castle.
You could use the money you earned as a down payment
and ask a bank to lend you the rest.

Then you would pay the bank back,
a little at a time, month after month . . .

for many years.

But the amount you must pay the bank
will be *more* than what you borrowed.
That's because the bank charges
for lending you money. The extra money
is called interest, just like the interest
the bank pays to you when it uses your money.
Now you are using the bank's money, so you must
pay interest to the bank.

If you have some very expensive plans,
you may have to take on a tough job
that pays well.

If you think ogre-taming would be
an exciting challenge, you can have fun
and make a great deal of money, too.
Of course, you may not enjoy
taming obstreperous ogres or building bulky bridges
or painting purple pots. Enjoying your work
is more important than money, so you should look
for another job or make less expensive plans.

CONGRATULATIONS! YOU'VE MADE A MILLION.

A MILLION DOLLARS!
That's a stack of pennies ninety-five miles high,
or enough nickels to fill a school bus,
or a whale's weight in quarters.

Would you prefer your million in paper money?
Even a paper million is a hefty load:
A million one-dollar bills would weigh 2,500 pounds
and stack up to 360 feet.

What's the smallest your million could be?
One-hundred-dollar bills are the largest made today,
and it would take ten thousand of them
to pay you for your feat of ogre-taming.
But a check for $1,000,000
would easily fit in your pocket or purse.
And it's worth the same as the towering stacks
of pennies or bills.

Now you can afford to buy tickets to the moon.

Or you can purchase some real estate
for the endangered rhinoceroses.

But if you'd rather save your million
than spend it, you could put it
in the bank, where it would earn interest.
The interest on a million is about $1,000 a week,
or $143 a day, or $6 an hour, or 10 cents a minute.
Just from sitting in the bank!

If you keep your million, you can probably live on the interest without doing any more work for the rest of your life. You might like that, or you could find it rather dull.

Making money means making choices.

SO WHAT WOULD YOU DO IF YOU MADE A MILLION?

Talking to David Schwartz

Ilene Cooper interviewed author David Schwartz.

Ilene Cooper: *Where did the idea for this book come from?*

David Schwartz: *If You Made a Million* grew from my earlier book about big numbers, *How Much Is a Million?* We see these big numbers in the newspaper every day, but very few of us understand them. So I wrote *How Much Is a Million?* After that book came out, people said, "We liked it, but you didn't talk about the kinds of millions we like best—millions of dollars!"

Cooper: *You've said you were always interested in big numbers. What did you mean by that?*

Schwartz: Let me give you an example. I've always liked the stars. I would look up at night and wonder how long it would take me to count them all. I also liked to take long bike rides. I would say, "Wow, this is a really long ride, but I wonder what it would be like to ride to Alpha Centauri, the nearest star." Alpha Centauri is more than four light years away. Light travels 186,000 miles per second. That's like going around the world seven times in one second. . . . Well, you see what I mean. I was always dealing with big numbers.

Cooper: *Do you plan to write more books about big numbers?*

Schwartz: Yes. I'm already working on a book about numbers beyond a million. It's going to combine math with one of my other great interests—nature.

Talking to
Steven Kellogg

Ilene Cooper interviewed illustrator Steven Kellogg.

Ilene Cooper: *Did you ever earn money from your art when you were a child?*

Steven Kellogg: As a matter of fact, I did. I would knock on people's doors and say, "I just drew a picture of your pet. Maybe you'd like to buy it." Some people did!

Cooper: *How did you feel about money when you were young?*

Kellogg: I found out pretty early on that it was good to have money in your pocket, so I was always getting jobs around the neighborhood. When I was old enough to ride my bike out of the neighborhood, I got a job with a woman who raised dogs. That was great because I love animals.

Cooper: *If You Made a Million is different from the other books you've done, isn't it?*

Kellogg: Yes! The book presented an interesting challenge—how do you illustrate a book that's mostly numbers? I thought the book needed a main character so I invented Marvelosissimo, the Mathematical Magician.

Response Corner

Spending and Saving

Saving is an important habit to learn. Plan a weekly budget. First, decide how much money you will start with. Next, figure out how much you need to spend and how much you can save. Then follow your plan!

WRITE AN AD

Wanted: Baby-sitter

Want ads in newspapers list jobs. Study the want ads in your newspaper. Now think of a job you would like someone to do, such as baby-sit your little brother or sister. Write an ad for the job, and post it in your classroom.

312

Career Interview

As you read in "If You Made a Million," how much money you earn depends on what kind of job you have. But money isn't the only thing to think about when choosing a job. Interview a family member about his or her work. Ask that person why he or she chose to do that kind of work.

★ What Do You Think? ★

- If you earned a lot of money, why might you want to save some of it in a bank rather than spend it all?

- What would be the best way to pay for something that cost a lot of money? Would you use coins, dollars, or a check? Explain your answer.

- How would you explain to someone from another planet what money is and what it is used for?

The King and the Poor Boy

A Cambodian folktale
retold by
Muriel Paskin Carrison
from a translation by the Venerable Kong Chhean

In a small village near the edge of the forest, there once lived a buffalo boy who had no mother or father. His uncle, who was the chief cook for the king, pitied the poor boy. So he invited the boy to stay with him in the palace. The grateful boy worked hard to help his uncle. He washed the plates, polished the cups, cleaned the dining room tables, and mopped the floors. At the end of each month, his uncle gave him six *sen*[1] as his wages.

Now the king frequently inspected the palace quarters. He often noticed the hardworking boy mopping the floors or polishing the cups, cheerfully and in good humor. One day the king asked the boy, "Do you receive wages for your hard work?"

---

[1] six *sen*: Cambodian money, worth about six cents

The boy bowed and said, "Yes, I do, Your Majesty. I earn six *sen* every month."

Then the king asked, "Do you think you are rich or do you think you are poor?"

"Your Majesty," the boy replied, "I think that I am as rich as a king."

The king was taken by surprise. "Why is this poor boy talking such nonsense?" he mused to himself.

Once more, the king spoke to the boy, "I am a king and I have all the power and riches of this country. You earn only six *sen* a month. Why do you say you are as rich as I am?"

The boy laid down his broom and slowly replied to the king, "Your Majesty, I may receive only six *sen* each month, but I eat from one plate and you also eat from one plate. I sleep for one night and you also sleep for one night. We eat and sleep the same. There is no difference. Now, Your Majesty, do you understand why I say that I am as rich as a king?"

The king understood and was satisfied.

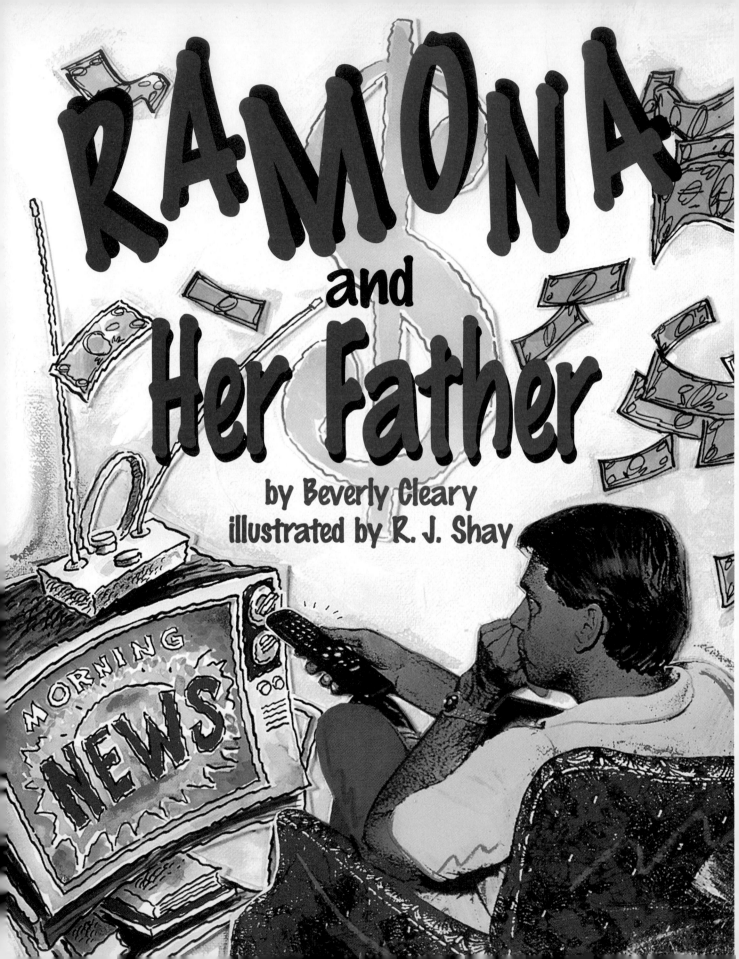

RAMONA
and
Her Father

by Beverly Cleary

illustrated by R. J. Shay

Ever since Mr. Quimby lost his job, Ramona has been wondering if he is too worried to love her anymore. He certainly isn't any fun these days. Ramona decides to solve the family's problems by earning a million dollars. She figures she can do this by starring in a television commercial. She has seen kids on TV do things like eat margarine and wear silly crowns. One girl even told her mom that her pantyhose looked like elephant legs, and she didn't get into trouble. Ramona is sure she can do these things and more. So she starts practicing. . . .

Ramona continued to practice until she began to feel as if a television camera was watching her wherever she went. She smiled a lot and skipped, feeling that she was cute and lovable. She felt as if she had fluffy blond curls, even though in real life her hair was brown and straight.

One morning, smiling prettily, she thought, and swinging her lunch box, Ramona skipped to school. Today someone might notice her because she was wearing her red tights. She was happy because this was a special day, the day of Ramona's parent-teacher conference. Since Mrs. Quimby was at work, Mr. Quimby was going to meet with Mrs. Rogers, her second-grade teacher. Ramona was proud to have a father who would come to school.

Feeling dainty, curly-haired, and adorable, Ramona skipped into her classroom, and what did she see but Mrs. Rogers with wrinkles around her ankles. Ramona did not hesitate. She skipped right over to her teacher and, since there did not happen to be an elephant in Room 2, turned the words around and said, "Mrs. Rogers, your pantyhose are wrinkled like an elephant's legs."

Mrs. Rogers looked surprised, and the boys and girls who had already taken their seats giggled. All the teacher said was, "Thank you, Ramona, for telling me. And remember, we do not skip inside the school building."

Ramona had an uneasy feeling she had displeased her teacher.

She was sure of it when Howie said, "Ramona, you sure weren't very polite to Mrs. Rogers." Howie, a serious thinker, was usually right.

Suddenly Ramona was no longer an adorable little fluffy-haired girl on television. She was plain old Ramona, a second-grader whose own red tights bagged at the knee and wrinkled at the ankle. This wasn't the way things turned out on television. On television grown-ups always smiled at everything children said.

During recess Ramona went to the girls' bathroom and rolled her tights up at the waist to stretch them up at the knee and ankle. Mrs. Rogers must have done the same thing to her pantyhose, because after recess her ankles were smooth. Ramona felt better.

That afternoon, when the lower grades had been dismissed from their classrooms, Ramona found her father, along with Davy's mother, waiting outside the door of Room 2 for their conferences with Mrs. Rogers. Davy's mother's appointment was first, so Mr. Quimby sat down on a chair outside the door with a folder of Ramona's schoolwork to look over. Davy stood close to the door, hoping to hear what his teacher was saying about him. Everybody in Room 2 was anxious to learn what the teacher said.

Mr. Quimby opened Ramona's folder. "Run along and play on the playground until I'm through," he told his daughter.

"Promise you'll tell me what Mrs. Rogers says about me," said Ramona.

Mr. Quimby understood. He smiled and gave his promise.

Outside, the playground was chilly and damp. The only children who lingered were those whose parents had conferences, and they were more interested in what was going on inside the building than outside. Bored, Ramona looked around for something to do, and because she could find nothing better, she followed a traffic boy across the street. On the opposite side, near the market that had been built when she was in kindergarten, she decided she had time to explore. In a weedy space at the side of the market building, she discovered several burdock plants that bore a prickly crop of brown burs, each covered with sharp, little hooks.

Ramona saw at once that burs had all sorts of interesting possibilities. She picked two and stuck them together. She added another and another. They were better than Tinker-toys. She would have to tell Howie about them. When she had a string of burs, each clinging to the next, she bent it into a circle and stuck the ends together. A crown! She could make a crown. She picked more burs and built up the circle by making peaks all the way around like the crown the boy wore in the margarine commercial. There was only one thing to do with a crown like that. Ramona crowned herself—ta-*da*!—like the boy on television.

Prickly though it was, Ramona enjoyed wearing the crown. She practiced looking surprised, like the boy who ate the margarine, and pretended she was rich and famous and about to meet her father, who would be driving a big shiny car bought with the million dollars she had earned.

The traffic boys had gone off duty. Ramona remembered to look both ways before she crossed the street, and as she crossed she pretended people were saying, "There goes that rich girl. She earned a million dollars eating margarine on TV."

Mr. Quimby was standing on the playground, looking for Ramona. Forgetting all she had been pretending, Ramona ran to him. "What did Mrs. Rogers say about me?" she demanded.

"That's some crown you've got there," Mr. Quimby remarked.

"Daddy, what did she *say*?" Ramona could not contain her impatience.

Mr. Quimby grinned. "She said you were impatient."

Oh, that. People were always telling Ramona not to be so impatient. "What else?" asked Ramona, as she and her father walked toward home.

"You are a good reader, but you are careless about spelling."

Ramona knew this. Unlike Beezus, who was an excellent speller, Ramona could not believe spelling was important as long as people could understand what she meant. "What else?"

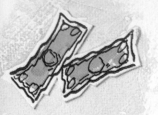

"She said you draw unusually well for a second-grader and your printing is the best in the class."

"What else?"

Mr. Quimby raised one eyebrow as he looked down at Ramona. "She said you were inclined to show off and you sometimes forget your manners."

Ramona was indignant at this criticism. "I do not! She's just making that up." Then she remembered what she had said about her teacher's pantyhose and felt subdued. She hoped her teacher had not repeated her remark to her father.

"I remember my manners most of the time," said Ramona, wondering what her teacher had meant by showing off. Being first to raise her hand when she knew the answer?

"Of course you do," agreed Mr. Quimby. "After all, you are my daughter. Now tell me, how are you going to get that crown off?"

Using both hands, Ramona tried to lift her crown but only succeeded in pulling her hair. The tiny hooks clung fast. Ramona tugged. Ow! That hurt. She looked helplessly up at her father.

Mr. Quimby appeared amused. "Who do you think you are? A Rose Festival Queen?"

Ramona pretended to ignore her father's question. How silly to act like someone on television when she was a plain old second-grader whose tights bagged at the knees again. She hoped her father would not guess. He might. He was good at guessing.

By then Ramona and her father were home. As Mr. Quimby unlocked the front door, he said, "We'll have to see what we can do about getting you uncrowned before your mother gets home. Any ideas?"

Ramona had no answer, although she was eager to part with the crown before her father guessed what she had been doing. In the kitchen, Mr. Quimby picked off the top of the crown, the part that did not touch Ramona's hair. That was easy. Now came the hard part.

"Yow!" said Ramona, when her father tried to lift the crown.

"That won't work," said her father. "Let's try one bur at a time." He went to work on one bur, carefully trying to untangle it from Ramona's hair, one strand at a time. To Ramona, who did not like to stand still, this process took forever. Each bur was snarled in a hundred hairs, and each hair had to be pulled before the bur was loosened. After a very long time, Mr. Quimby handed a hair-entangled bur to Ramona.

"Yow! Yipe! Leave me some hair," said Ramona, picturing a bald circle around her head.

"I'm trying," said Mr. Quimby and began on the next bur.

Ramona sighed. Standing still doing nothing was tiresome.

After what seemed like a long time, Beezus came home from school. She took one look at Ramona and began to laugh.

"I don't suppose you ever did anything dumb," said Ramona, short of patience and anxious lest her sister guess why she was wearing the remains of a crown. "What about the time you—"

"No arguments," said Mr. Quimby. "We have a problem to solve, and it might be a good idea if we solved it before your mother comes home from work."

Much to Ramona's annoyance, her sister sat down to watch. "How about soaking?" suggested Beezus. "It might soften all those millions of little hooks."

"Yow! Yipe!" said Ramona. "You're pulling too hard."

Mr. Quimby laid another hair-filled bur on the table. "Maybe we should try. This isn't working."

"It's about time she washed her hair anyway," said Beezus, a remark Ramona felt was entirely unnecessary. Nobody could shampoo hair full of burs.

Ramona knelt on a chair with her head in a sinkful of warm water for what seemed like hours until her knees ached and she had a crick in her neck. "Now, Daddy?" she asked at least once a minute.

"Not yet," Mr. Quimby answered, feeling a bur. "Nope," he said at last. "This isn't going to work."

Ramona lifted her dripping head from the sink. When her father tried to dry her hair, the bur hooks clung to the towel. He jerked the towel loose and draped it around Ramona's shoulders.

"Well, live and learn," said Mr. Quimby. "Beezus, scrub some potatoes and throw them in the oven. We can't have your mother come home and find we haven't started supper."

When Mrs. Quimby arrived, she took one look at her husband trying to untangle Ramona's wet hair from the burs, groaned, sank limply onto a kitchen chair, and began to laugh.

By now Ramona was tired, cross, and hungry. "I don't see anything funny," she said sullenly.

Mrs. Quimby managed to stop laughing. "What on earth got into you?" she asked.

Ramona considered. Was this a question grown-ups asked just to be asking a question, or did her mother expect an answer? "Nothing," was a safe reply. She would never tell her family how she happened to be wearing a crown of burs. Never, not even if they threw her into a dungeon.

"Beezus, bring me the scissors," said Mrs. Quimby.

Ramona clapped her hands over the burs. "No!" she shrieked and stamped her foot. "I won't let you cut off my hair! I won't! I won't! I won't!"

Beezus handed her mother the scissors and gave her sister some advice. "Stop yelling. If you go to bed with burs in your hair, you'll really get messed up."

Ramona had to face the wisdom of Beezus's words. She stopped yelling to consider the problem once more. "All right," she said, as if she were granting a favor, "but I want Daddy to do it." Her father would work with care while her mother, always in a hurry since she was working full time, would go *snip-snip-snip* and be done with it. Besides, supper would be prepared faster and would taste better if her mother did the cooking.

"I am honored," said Mr. Quimby. "Deeply honored."

Mrs. Quimby did not seem sorry to hand over the scissors. "Why don't you go someplace else to work while Beezus and I get supper on the table?"

Mr. Quimby led Ramona into the living room, where he turned on the television set. "This may take time," he exclaimed, as he went to work. "We might as well watch the news."

Ramona was still anxious. "Don't cut any more than you have to, Daddy," she begged, praying the margarine boy would not appear on the screen. "I don't want everyone at school to make fun of me." The newscaster was talking about strikes and a lot of things Ramona did not understand.

"The merest smidgin," promised her father. *Snip. Snip. Snip.* He laid a hair-ensnarled bur in an ashtray. *Snip. Snip. Snip.* He laid another bur beside the first.

"Does it look awful?" asked Ramona.

"As my grandmother would say, 'It will never be noticed from a trotting horse.'"

Ramona let out a long, shuddery sigh, the closest thing to crying without really crying. *Snip. Snip. Snip.* Ramona touched the side of her head. She still had hair there. More hair than she expected. She felt a little better.

The newscaster disappeared from the television screen, and there was that boy again singing:

FORGET YOUR POTS,
FORGET YOUR PANS.
IT'S NOT TOO LATE
TO CHANGE YOUR
PLANS.

Ramona thought longingly of the days before her father lost his job, when they could forget their pots and pans and change their plans. She watched the boy open his mouth wide and sink his teeth into that fat hamburger with lettuce, tomato, and cheese hanging out of the bun. She swallowed and said, "I bet that boy has a lot of fun with his million dollars." She felt so sad. The Quimbys really needed a million dollars. Even one dollar would help.

327

Snip. Snip. Snip. "Oh, I don't know," said Mr. Quimby. "Money is handy, but it isn't everything."

"I wish I could earn a million dollars like that boy," said Ramona. This was the closest she would ever come to telling how she happened to set a crown of burs on her head.

"You know something?" said Mr. Quimby. "I don't care how much that kid or any other kid earns. I wouldn't trade you for a million dollars."

"Really, Daddy?" That remark about any other kid—Ramona wondered if her father had guessed her reason for the crown, but she would never ask. Never. "Really? Do you mean it?"

"Really." Mr. Quimby continued his careful snipping. "I'll bet that boy's father wishes he had a little girl who finger-painted and wiped her hands on the cat when she was little and who once cut her own hair so she would be bald like her uncle and who then grew up to be seven years old and crowned herself with burs. Not every father is lucky enough to have a daughter like that."

Ramona giggled. "Daddy, you're being silly!" She was happier than she had been in a long time.

a conversation with
Beverly Cleary

How does Beverly Cleary write? Read this interview to find out.

Ilene Cooper: How do you actually do your writing?

Beverly Cleary: Oh, I write with a pen first. Then I type up what I've written so I can see what it looks like.

Cooper: What is the hardest thing about writing for you, and what is the easiest thing?

Cleary: The hardest thing about writing is pushing through to the end of the story. The easiest thing is revising. I think all writers do some revising. That's when I cross out a lot and shorten a page to one paragraph.

Cooper: When you start a book, do you know how it's going to end?

Cleary: In *Ramona and Her Father*, I wrote the last chapter first. It began as a short story, a Christmas story, I was asked to write for a magazine. And as I wrote it, I began to think about how the family got to this point. In a way, I wrote that book backwards. I often begin in the middle. I begin with the characters and something they would do and just let the story work itself out.

MAKE A CHART

The Travelin' Burs

The burs that Ramona used for her crown became a thorny problem. Many seeds have unusual ways of traveling from a flower to a place where they can grow. In a science book or an encyclopedia, find out about some of these seeds. On a chart, name the seeds, explain how they travel, and draw a picture of each one.

RESPONSE

MAKE A LIST

Odd Jobs Needed

Ramona wanted to help her family by working in a television commercial. What jobs could a young person like Ramona really do? List your ideas. Include ways that Ramona could help in her own home, without being paid.

I'll Buy That!

Television commercials are a type of advertisement. Advertisements try to get people to buy things. For one or two days, pay special attention to all the advertisements you see and hear, and take notes. What are the people in each advertisement like? Does the ad use many words or just a few? How many times is the name of the product used? Compare your notes with a classmate.

CORNER

What Do You Think?

- At the end of the story, Ramona is happier than she's been in a long time. Why has her mood changed?

- What do you like most about Ramona? What do you like least?

- Ramona learns a lesson about what is really important in life. How important is money in your life? Are there other things that are more important to you? Explain.

Theme Wrap-Up

Creating a new invention is a challenge. Doing a job that helps someone is another kind of challenge. Which of the challenges in this theme do you think would be the most exciting? Why?

If Ramona ever does make a million dollars, what do you think she should do with it? Think about the selection "If You Made a Million" to help you answer.

Activity Corner

Hold a classroom science fair. Ask several students to work on projects, inventions, and experiments to show at the fair. Invite people from other classes to visit the fair.

Glossary

WHAT IS A GLOSSARY?

A glossary is like a small dictionary at the back of a book. It lists some of the words used in the book, along with their pronunciations, their meanings, and other useful information. If you come across a word you don't know as you are reading, you can look up the word in this glossary.

Using the

Like a dictionary, this glossary lists words in alphabetical order. To find a word, look it up by its first letter or letters.

To save time, use the **guide words** at the top of each page. These show you the first and last words on the page. Look at the guide words to see if your word falls between them alphabetically.

Here is an example of a glossary entry:

> This is the entry word. It's the word you look up.

> Look here to find out how to pronounce the word.

> The letter *n.* means the entry word is a noun.

> Here you'll find other forms of the word.

com·bi·na·tion
[kom´bə·nā´shən] *n.* **com·bi·na·tions** A way things are put together: **Fruit juices come in many different *combinations*, such as cranberry and apple or orange and pineapple.** *syn.* mixture

> This is the definition of the entry word.

> This is a sample sentence using the entry word.

> Synonyms of the entry word come right after *syn.*

ETYMOLOGY

Etymology is the study or history of how words are developed. Words often have interesting backgrounds that can help you remember what they mean. Look in the margins of the glossary to find the etymologies of certain words.

Here is an example of an etymology:

value   The Latin word *valēre* means "to be strong." The Old French language used this word to make the word *value*, changing the meaning to "worth."

Glossary

PRONUNCIATION

The pronunciation in brackets is a respelling that shows how the word is pronounced.

The **pronunciation key** explains what the symbols in a respelling mean. A shortened pronunciation key appears on every other page of the glossary.

PRONUNCIATION KEY*

a	add, map	m	move, seem	u	up, done
ā	ace, rate	n	nice, tin	û(r)	burn, term
â(r)	care, air	ng	ring, song	yo͞o	fuse, few
ä	palm, father	o	odd, hot	v	vain, eve
b	bat, rub	ō	open, so	w	win, away
ch	check, catch	ô	order, jaw	y	yet, yearn
d	dog, rod	oi	oil, boy	z	zest, muse
e	end, pet	ou	pout, now	zh	vision, pleasure
ē	equal, tree	o͝o	took, full	ə	the schwa, an
f	fit, half	o͞o	pool, food		unstressed vowel
g	go, log	p	pit, stop		representing the
h	hope, hate	r	run, poor		sound spelled
i	it, give	s	see, pass		*a* in *above*
ī	ice, write	sh	sure, rush		*e* in *sicken*
j	joy, ledge	t	talk, sit		*i* in *possible*
k	cool, take	th	thin, both		*o* in *melon*
l	look, rule	t̶h̶	this, bathe		*u* in *circus*

Other symbols:
- • separates words into syllables
- ´ indicates heavier stress on a syllable
- ` indicates light stress on a syllable

Abbreviations: *adj.* adjective, *adv.* adverb, *conj.* conjunction, *interj.* interjection, *n.* noun, *prep.* preposition, *pron.* pronoun, *syn.* synonym, *v.* verb.

amount
Amount comes from the Latin word meaning "to the mountain" or "upward." An *amount* may be the total number when counting upward or adding.

af·fect
[ə·fekt´] *v.* **af·fects**
To change; to cause something else to happen: **This experiment shows how sunlight *affects* the growth of plants.** *syn.* influence

al·low·ance
[ə·lou´əns] *n.* A set sum of money a person gets regularly, such as each week: **Gordon gets an *allowance* of five dollars every week.**

a·mount
[ə·mount´] *n.* A certain number of something; a sum: **The *amount* of money I had was not enough to buy the poster.** *syn.* quantity

anx·ious
[angk´shəs] *adj.* Worried; uneasy: **Valerie was *anxious* about oversleeping because she thought she might miss the school bus.**

ar·rive
[ə·rīv´] *v.* **ar·rived** To get to a place: **Ivan *arrived* at the game at four o'clock.** *syn.* reach

as·ton·ish
[ə·ston´ish] *v.* **as·ton·ished** To surprise; to fill with wonder: **It was a clear night, and the number of stars in the sky *astonished* him.** *syn.* amaze

blind
[blīnd] *adj.* Unable to see: **Most fish that live in dark caves are *blind*.**

brace

[brās] *v.* **braced** To prepare for something that might be bad; to hold oneself tightly in place: **Ryan held onto a pole on the bus as he *braced* himself for a sudden stop.**

buck•et

[buk´it] *n.* **buck•ets** A round container with a flat bottom and a curved handle, used to carry things: **Shelly filled two *buckets* with water, got some soap and a mop, and was ready to wash the floor.** *syn.* pail

cab•in

[kab´in] *n.* A small wooden house, sometimes made of big logs: **Our family stays in a *cabin* by a lake every summer.** *syn.* hut

car•pen•ter

[kär´pən•tər] *n.* A person who makes things out of wood: **The *carpenter* made a bookcase for our room.**

child•hood

[chīld´hŏŏd´] *n.* The time when someone is young: **Tara had a very happy *childhood* and always played with her friends.** *syn.* youth

choice

[chois] *n.* **choic•es** The act of picking which one: **There were many *choices* to make at the bakery, but we decided to get muffins and apple tarts.** *syns.* decision, selection

bucket The Old English word *buc* also means "belly." A *bucket* is a container that holds things, just as a belly is a container that holds food.

cabin

a	add	ŏŏ	took
ā	ace	ōō	pool
â	care	u	up
ä	palm	û	burn
e	end	yōō	fuse
ē	equal	oi	oil
i	it	ou	pout
ī	ice	ng	ring
o	odd	th	thin
ō	open	t̶h̶	this
ô	order	zh	vision

$$\schwa = \begin{cases} a \text{ in } above \\ e \text{ in } sicken \\ i \text{ in } possible \\ o \text{ in } melon \\ u \text{ in } circus \end{cases}$$

comfortable
This word comes from *comfort*, which used to mean "strong." In the 1800s, its meaning changed and became "at ease."

creek

com·bi·na·tion
[kom′bə·nā′shən] *n.*
com·bi·na·tions A way things are put together: **Fruit juices come in many different *combinations*, such as cranberry and apple or orange and pineapple.** *syn.* mixture

com·fort·a·ble
[kum′fər·tə·bəl] *adj.*
Restful; at ease: **In the summer, José feels *comfortable* in his air-conditioned house.**

com·mer·cial
[kə·mûr′shəl] *n.* An advertisement on television or radio, used for selling something: **The *commercial* for the new cereal made Kelly feel hungry.**

con·grat·u·la·tions
[kən·grach′ə·lā′shənz] *n.* Good wishes letting someone know you are happy for him or her: **Congratulations on your team's great game!**

crea·ture
[krē′chər] *n.* **crea·tures** An animal: **Many different *creatures* live in the rain forest.**

creek
[krēk or krik] *n.* A small, narrow river that may not be very deep: **The cowboy got fresh water for his horse from the *creek*.** *syn.* stream

cu·ri·ous
[kyoŏr′ē·əs] *adj.* Wanting to know or find out more: **Elena was *curious* and wanted to learn how rainbows are formed.** *syn.* questioning

D

depth

[depth] *n.* **depths** A far distance into something; the part deep down: **The sunken ship was lost in the *depths* of the sea.**

des·ti·na·tion

[des´tə·nā´shən] *n.* The place someone is going to; a goal: **The *destination* of our trip was New York City, and we were eager to get there.**

de·stroy

[di·stroi´] *v.* **de·stroyed** To put an end to; to break something apart so badly that it cannot be fixed: **After the storm, our garden was *destroyed* and we had to replant everything.** *syns.* ruin, wreck

dor·mant

[dôr´mənt] *adj.* Not moving or growing for a period of time; at rest: **The plants under the snow are *dormant*, but they will grow again in the spring.** *syn.* asleep

E

earn

[ûrn] *v.* **earned** To get as payment for hard work: **Han *earned* some money by washing cars.** *syn.* gain

ech·o

[ek´ō] *n.* **ech·oes** A sound that comes back again: **Tommy shouted into the cave and heard the *echoes* of his voice come back softer and softer, again and again.** *syn.* repetition

depths *Depth* comes from the word *deep*. *Deep* comes from a word that means "diving duck." Many words have come from *deep*, such as *dimple*, *dip*, and *dive*.

earn

a	add	o͝o	took
ā	ace	o͞o	pool
â	care	u	up
ä	palm	û	burn
e	end	yo͞o	fuse
ē	equal	oi	oil
i	it	ou	pout
ī	ice	ng	ring
o	odd	th	thin
ō	open	th	this
ô	order	zh	vision

ə = {
a in *above*
e in *sicken*
i in *possible*
o in *melon*
u in *circus*
}

graze

hesitate
Hesitate once
meant "to
become stuck."
It now means "to
pause or wait."

em•per•or
[em´pər•ər] *n.* A person who rules a land: **The *emperor* lived in a beautiful palace, and he made all the laws himself.** *syn.* king

en•er•gy
[en´ər•jē] *n.* The force or power to make things work; the ability to make things go: **Eating breakfast in the morning gives me *energy* to work during the day.**

ex•ist
[ig•zist´] *v.* To be; to live: **Dinosaurs do not *exist* anymore, but we can learn about them in books.**

ex•tinc•tion
[ik•stingk´shən] *n.* When there is no more of a kind of animal or plant: **The white tigers in India are faced with *extinction* because people have hunted them too much.**

G

graze
[grāz] *v.* **graz•ing** To feed on grass: **The cows were *grazing* on the hillside where the grass was thick.**

H

hes•i•tate
[hez´ə•tāt´] *v.* To stop and think whether to do or say something: **Carol saw her father *hesitate* before he bought the purple lamp.** *syns.* pause, delay

home•sick
[hōm´sik´] *adj.* Sad because you miss your family and the place you live: **Aretha was very *homesick* while she was at overnight camp.** *syn.* lonely

 **I**

i·den·ti·fy

[ī·den´tə·fī´] *v.*
i·den·ti·fied To see and know by name; to point out: **Julian *identified* three butterflies while on a field trip to the park.** *syn.* recognize

im·age

[im´ij] *n.* A picture or likeness of, as seen in a mirror: **Katy saw her *image* reflected in the store window.** *syn.* appearance

im·pa·tience

[im·pā´shəns] *n.* A feeling of not wanting to wait; not wanting things to slow down: **Sam made a mistake on the test because of his *impatience* to be the first one done.** *syn.* eagerness

L

ledge

[lej] *n.* A narrow, flat shelf that sticks out from a steep rock or wall: **Carlos put some flower-pots on the *ledge* outside the window.**

M

man·ners

[man´ərz] *n.* Polite ways to do things; ways to do things that show good behavior: **My mother taught me the good *manners* to always say "Please" and "Thank you."** *syn.* etiquette

mol·ten

[mōl´tən] *adj.* Made into a hot liquid by heat: **When a volcano becomes active, *molten* rock, or lava, flows out of it.**

molten *Molten* is from the word *melt.* The first meaning of *melt* was "soft." When something *melts,* it usually becomes a liquid or a "soft" substance.

a	add	o͝o	took
ā	ace	o͞o	pool
â	care	u	up
ä	palm	û	burn
e	end	yo͞o	fuse
ē	equal	oi	oil
i	it	ou	pout
ī	ice	ng	ring
o	odd	th	thin
ō	open	th	this
ô	order	zh	vision

ə = {
 a in *above*
 e in *sicken*
 i in *possible*
 o in *melon*
 u in *circus*
}

peculiar
Peculiar comes from a Latin word meaning "private property." *Pecu* meant "cattle," and years ago cattle were very important property. The meaning then changed to "belonging only to oneself." In English, it came to mean "being the only one of its kind."

N

ner•vous

[nûr´vəs] *adj.* Worried and somewhat fearful: **I felt *nervous* about singing in front of the class, but I did it anyway.** *syn.* uneasy

or•bit

[ôr´bit] *v.* **orbits** To move around another object, usually in space: **The Earth *orbits* the sun once a year.** *syn.* circle

P

pave

[pāv] *v.* **paved** To cover an area of ground with something hard, such as concrete: **The street in front of my house was once dirt, but it was *paved* last week.**

pe•cul•iar

[pi•kyo͞ol´yər] *adj.* Belonging to only one person or thing; strange or unusual: **Jennifer had a *peculiar* dog that ate carrots.** *syns.* unique, odd

peer

[pir] *v.* **peer•ing** To look closer to see more clearly: **Billy was *peering* under the bed, looking for his shoes.**

pop·u·la·tion
[pop´yə·lā´shən] *n.*
pop·u·la·tions A group
or kind; a certain group
of people or animals
living in one place:
**Some owl *populations*
are in danger because
people are cutting
down too many of the
trees that they live in.**
syn. inhabitants

post·card
[pōst´kärd´] *n.*
post·cards A stiff,
rectangular piece of
paper with a picture on
one side and writing
space on the other
side, made to be sent
through the mail: **While
Carmen was traveling
with her parents, she
kept in touch with her
friends by sending
them *postcards*.**

re·ceive
[ri·sēv´] *v.* To get
something, as in a gift: **I
will *receive* 5 cents for
every soda can I turn in.**
syns. acquire, obtain

re·mind
[ri·mīnd´] *v.* **re·mind·ed**
To cause to remember;
to make someone think
of something again: **The
tacos *reminded* Jane of
her trip to Mexico and
of the wonderful food
she ate there.**

sax·o·phone
[sak´sə·fōn´] *n.* A musical
instrument in the shape
of a curved brass tube:
**Mike plays a *saxophone*
in the band.**

saxophone

a	add	o͝o	took
ā	ace	o͞o	pool
â	care	u	up
ä	palm	û	burn
e	end	yo͞o	fuse
ē	equal	oi	oil
i	it	ou	pout
ī	ice	ng	ring
o	odd	th	thin
ō	open	t͟h	this
ô	order	zh	vision

ə = {
a in *above*
e in *sicken*
i in *possible*
o in *melon*
u in *circus*

343

soldier The Latin word *solidus* means "military pay." French changed it to *solde*, and the person getting the military pay was called a *soldior*. English changed it to *soldier*.

soldier

sea•coast

[sē´kōst´] *n.* The area where the land meets the ocean: **When walking along the *seacoast*, it is fun to watch the waves.** *syns.* shore, beach

silk

[silk] *n.* A kind of cloth made from a strong, shiny, threadlike material: **Suki likes scarves made of *silk* because they feel so smooth.**

sol•dier

[sōl´jər] *n.* **sol•diers** A person in the army; someone who watches over others and keeps them from harm: **The *soldiers* guard the queen when she is outside the palace.** *syns.* protector, fighter

spy

[spī] *v.* To watch closely without being seen: **The little kids always *spy* on us because they want to find our secret clubhouse.**

sur•face

[sûr´fis] *n.* The outer part of something; the outer layer that covers something: **The *surface* of the moon is rocky and dry.**

sur•vive

[sər•vīv´] *v.* To live through; to stay alive: **Dolphins need to come up for air in order to *survive* in the ocean.** *syn.* remain

swal•low

[swol´ō] *v.* To make something go down the throat and into the stomach: **I try to chew my food well, so it will be easy to *swallow*.**

tame

[tām] *adj.* Under control, not wild: **The *tame* animals in the petting zoo will not bite.**
syn. gentle

throne

[thrōn] *n.* A chair for a ruler: **The king sat on his *throne* as the crown was placed on his head.**

un·der·ground

[un´dər·ground´] *adj.* Below the earth: **We went into the tunnel and rode the *underground* train.**

uni·verse

[yōō´nə·vûrs´] *n.* Everything in the world; the sun, stars, and planets: **Astronauts see parts of the *universe* that cannot be seen from Earth.**

val·ue

[val´yōō] *n.* The worth; the price: **This painting has great *value* because the painter is famous.**
syn. cost

view

[vyōō] *n.* What can be seen from a place: **I have a *view* of the street from my window.**

yawn

[yôn] *v.* To open the mouth wide when one is sleepy: **Tyrone was sleepy and he soon began to *yawn*.**

throne

value   The Latin word *valēre* means "to be strong." The Old French language used this word to make the word *value*, changing the meaning to "worth."

a	add	oŏ	took
ā	ace	ōō	pool
â	care	u	up
ä	palm	û	burn
e	end	yōō	fuse
ē	equal	oi	oil
i	it	ou	pout
ī	ice	ng	ring
o	odd	th	thin
ō	open	~~th~~	this
ô	order	zh	vision

ə = {
a in *above*
e in *sicken*
i in *possible*
o in *melon*
u in *circus*
}

INDEX OF
Titles and Authors

Page numbers in color refer to biographical information.

Acknowledgments

For permission to reprint copyrighted material, grateful acknowledgment is made to the following sources:

Beautiful America Publishing Company: Cover illustration by Carol Johnson from *A Journey of Hope/Una Jornada de Esperanza* by Bob Harvey and Diane Kelsay Harvey. Copyright 1991 by Little America Publishing Co.

Curtis Brown Ltd.: Corrected galley from *Borreguita and the Coyote* by Verna Aardema. Originally published in *A Bookworm Who Hatched*, Richard C. Owen Publishers, Inc., 1993.

Children's Television Workshop: "Patently Ridiculous" by Saul T. Prince, illustrated by John Lawrence/Bernstein & Associates from *3-2-1 Contact Magazine*, May 1994. Copyright 1994 by Children's Television Workshop. "A Class Act" from Kid City Magazine, March 1993. Text copyright 1993 by Children's Television Workshop.

Dial Books for Young Readers, a division of Penguin Books USA Inc.: Cover illustration by Jerry Pinkney from *Back Home* by Gloria Jean Pinkney. Illustration copyright © 1992 by Jerry Pinkney.

Dutton Signet, a division of Penguin Books USA Inc.: From *Nature's Great Balancing Act in Our Own Backyard* by E. Jaediker Norsgaard, photographs by Campbell Norsgaard. Text copyright © 1990 by E. Jaediker Norsgaard; photographs copyright © 1990 by Campbell Norsgaard.

Fitzhenry & Whiteside, Limited, Markham, Ontario: *Wolf Island* by Celia Godkin. Copyright © 1989 by Celia Godkin.

Greenwillow Books, a division of William Morrow & Company, Inc.: Cover illustration by Jim Fowler from *Dolphin Adventure: A True Story* by Wayne Grover. Illustration copyright © 1990 by Jim Fowler. "I Am Flying" from *The New Kid on the Block* by Jack Prelutsky, cover illustration by James Stevenson. Text copyright © 1984 by Jack Prelutsky; cover illustration copyright © 1984 by James Stevenson.

Grosset & Dunlap, Inc., a division of The Putnam & Grosset Group: Cover illustration by Paige Billin-Frye from *What's Out There? A Book About Space* by Lynn Wilson. Illustration copyright © 1993 by Paige Billin-Frye.

Harcourt Brace & Company: Cover illustration by Greg Shed from *Dandelions* by Eve Bunting. Illustration copyright © 1995 by Greg Shed. *The Lotus Seed* by Sherry Garland, illustrated by Tatsuro Kiuchi. Text copyright © 1993 by Sherry Garland; illustrations copyright © 1993 by Tatsuro Kiuchi.

HarperCollins Publishers: My Great-Aunt Arizona by Gloria Houston, illustrated by Susan Condie Lamb. Text copyright © 1992 by Gloria Houston; illustrations copyright © 1992 by Susan Condie Lamb. "A Bug Sat in a Silver Flower" from *Dogs & Dragons, Trees & Dreams* by Karla Kuskin. Text copyright © 1980 by Karla Kuskin. Cover illustration by Kam Mak from *The Year of the Panda* by Miriam Schlein. Illustration copyright © 1990 by Kam Mak.

Holiday House, Inc.: *Wolves* by Gail Gibbons. Copyright © 1994 by Gail Gibbons.

Henry Holt and Company: Cover illustration by Cat Bowman Smith from *Max Malone Makes a Million* by Charlotte Herman. Illustration copyright © 1991 by Catherine Bowman Smith.

Houghton Mifflin Company: Cover illustration by Karen M. Dugan from *Halmoni and the Picnic* by Sook Nyul Choi. Illustration copyright © 1993 by Karen Milone Dugan. *When Jo Louis Won the Title* by Belinda Rochelle, illustrated by Larry Johnson. Text copyright © 1994 by Belinda Rochelle; illustrations copyright © 1994 by Larry Johnson. *Grandfather's Journey* by Allen Say. Copyright © 1993 by Allen Say.

Hyperion Books For Children: *All Eyes on the Pond* by Michael J. Rosen, illustrated by Tom Leonard. Text copyright © 1994 by Michael J. Rosen; illustrations © 1994 by Tom Leonard.

Alfred A. Knopf, Inc.: *Borreguita and the Coyote* by Verna Aardema, illustrated by Petra Mathers. Text copyright © 1991 by Verna Aardema; illustrations copyright © 1991 by Petra Mathers.

Larousse Kingfisher Chambers Inc., New York: From *Our Universe: A Guide To What's Out There* (Retitled: "Journey Through the Solar System") by Russell Stannard, illustrated by Michael Bennallack-Hart, Helen Floate, and Diana Mayo. Text copyright © 1995 by Russell Stannard; illustrations copyright © 1995 by Larousse plc.

Lee & Low Books, Inc.: Cover illustration by Cornelius Van Wright and Ying-Hwa Hu from *Sam and the Lucky Money* by Karen Chinn. Illustration copyright © 1995 by Cornelius Van Wright and Ying-Hwa Hu.

Lerner Publications Company, Minneapolis, MN: Cover photograph by Jake Rajs from *The Statue of Liberty: America's Proud Lady* by Jim Haskins. Copyright © 1986 by Jim Haskins.

Lothrop, Lee & Shepard Books, a division of William Morrow & Company, Inc.: *If You Made a Million* by David M. Schwartz, illustrated by Steven Kellogg. Text copyright © 1989 by David M. Schwartz; illustrations copyright © 1989 by Steven Kellogg; photographs of money copyright © 1989 by George Ancona.

Morrow Junior Books, a division of William Morrow & Company, Inc.: From *Ramona and Her Father* by Beverly Cleary. Text copyright © 1975, 1977 by Beverly Cleary. Cover illustration by Louis Darling from *Ellen Tebbits* by Beverly Cleary. Copyright 1951 by Beverly Cleary. Cover illustration by Alan Tiegreen from *Ramona the Brave* by Beverly Cleary. Copyright © 1975 by Beverly Cleary. Cover illustration by Louis Darling from *The Mouse and the Motorcycle* by Beverly Cleary. Copyright © 1965 by Beverly Cleary. Cover illustration by Beatrice Darwin from *Socks* by Beverly Cleary. Copyright © 1973 by Beverly Cleary. Cover illustration by Louis Darling from *Henry and the Clubhouse* by Beverly Cleary. Copyright © 1962 by Beverly Cleary. Cover illustration by Louis Darling from *Otis Spofford* by Beverly Cleary. Copyright 1953 by Beverly Cleary. Cover illustration by Kay Life from *Muggie Maggie* by Beverly Cleary. Illustration copyright © 1990 by William Morrow and Company, Inc.

G. P. Putnam's Sons: From *Amber Brown Is Not a Crayon* by Paula Danziger, illustrated by Tony Ross. Text copyright © 1994 by Paula Danziger; illustrations copyright © 1994 by Tony Ross. Cover illustration by Tony Ross from *Amber Brown Goes Fourth* by Paula Danziger. Illustration copyright © 1995 by Tony Ross.

Random House, Inc.: Cover illustration by Dora Leder from *Julian's Glorious Summer* by Ann Cameron. Illustration copyright © 1987 by Dora Leder. Cover illustration by Arnold Lobel from *The Random House Book of Poetry for Children*, selected by Jack Prelutsky. Copyright © 1983 by Random House, Inc.

Marian Reiner, on behalf of Patricia Hubbell and Ju-Hong Chen: "The Inventor Thinks Up Helicopters" from *The Tigers Brought Pink Lemonade* by Patricia Hubbell, illustrated by Ju-Hong Chen. Text copyright © 1988 by Patricia Hubbell; illustrations copyright © 1988 by Ju-Hong Chen.

Scholastic Inc.: Cover illustration from *All About Alligators* by Jim Arnosky. Copyright © 1994 by Jim Arnosky. From My First Book of Biographies (Retitled: "Creative Minds at Work") by Jean Marzollo. Text copyright © 1994 by Jean Marzollo.

Charles E. Tuttle Company, Inc.: "The King and the Poor Boy" from *Cambodian Folk Stories from the Gatiloke*, retold by Muriel Paskin Carrison, from a translation by The Venerable Kong Chhean. Text © 1987 by Charles E. Tuttle Publishing Co., Inc.

Viking Penguin, a division of Penguin Books USA Inc.: Cover illustration by Susanna Natti from *Cam Jansen and the Mystery of the Television Dog* by David A. Adler. Illustration copyright © 1981 by Susanna Natti.

Dinh D. Vu: "Nothing that grows..."/"Hoa Sen" from *The Lotus Seed* by Sherry Garland.

Walker Books Limited, London: Cover illustration from *When Hunger Calls* by Bert Kitchen. Copyright © 1994 by Bert Kitchen. Originally published in the United States by Candlewick Press, Cambridge, MA.

Every effort has been made to locate the copyright holders for the selections in this work. The publishers would be pleased to receive information that would allow the corrections of any omissions in future printings.

Photo Credits

Key: (t) top, (b) bottom, (c) center, (l) left, (r) right, (bg) background, (i) inset

John Lei/OPC, 18, 55, 199(bg), 200-201; Melody Norsgaard/Newcombe Productions, 64-65; Herb Segars/Animals Animals. 68; Stephen Dalton/Photo Researchers, 70; Art Wolfe/Tony Stone Images, 71; Dwight Kuhn/Bruce Coleman, Inc., 72; Laura Riley/Bruce Coleman, Inc. 73(t), 77(b); E. R. Degginger/Animals Animals, 73(b); W. Bayer/Bruce Coleman, Inc., 74-75; S. Nielsen/Bruce Coleman, Inc, 76; Joe McDonald/Animals Animals, 77(t); Phil Degginger/Bruce Coleman, Inc., 78; Keith Gunnar/Bruce Coleman, Inc, 78-79; Robert P. Carr/Bruce Coleman, Inc., 79; Sal DiMarco/Black Star/Harcourt Brace & Company, 104; Wes Bobbitt/Black Star/Harcourt Brace & Company, 127; Culver Pictures, 130-131(bg), 160-161(bg), 164-165(bg); Dale Higgins/Harcourt Brace & Company, 160; Bob Newey, 199; Dennis Brack/Black Star/Harcourt Brace & Company, 217(t); Rick Friedman/Black Star/Harcourt Brace & Company, 217(b) Richard B. Levine, 218(t), Debra P. Hershkowitz, 218(b); Jeff Greenberg/Photo Researchers, 219(t), 219(b); Superstock, 226-227, 229(i), 230, 236-237, 239(i), 246-247(b), 260(bg); Earl Young/FPG International, 228-229; Telegraph Colour Library/FPG International, 233, 234-235, 260(b); NASA, 235(i), 238-239, 243-245, 246, 247(b), 248-253, 261(t), 261(c). 261(b); David Hardy/Photo researchers, 254; the Bettmann Archive, 269, 271; Les Morsillo, 274-279

Illustration Credits

Gennady Spirin, Cover Art; Lori Lohstoeder, 6-7, 13-17, 108; Margaret Kasahara, 8-9, 109-110, 113, 220; Wayne Vincent, 10-11, 221-225, 332; Tyrone Geter, title page; Lehner & White, misc. icons; Petra Mathers, 18-37; Gail Gibbons, 38-51; Celia Godkin, 54-63; Tom Leonard, 64-69, 86-87, 92-93, 258-259; Kristin Goeters, 69; Daniel Moreton, 80-81; Tom Leonard, 84-107; Susan Condie Lamb, 114-129; Allen Say, 130-161, 164-165; Arvis Stewart, 161; Tatsuro Kiuchi, 166-187; Paula Danziger, 190-198, 200-201; Larry Johnson, 202-217; Tyrone Geter, 217; Tom Leonard, 256-257; Ju-Hong Chen, 258-295; Hugh Whyte, 268-271; Steven Kellogg, 278-313; R.J. Shay, 316-331